ROSE ELLIOT'S
VEGETARIAN
F·A·S·T·F·O·O·D

ROSE ELLIOT'S
VEGETARIAN
F·A·S·T·F·O·O·D

Over 200 Delicious Dishes in Minutes

Random House
New York

ACKNOWLEDGEMENTS

My very grateful thanks to all the people who have been involved in the
production of this book; to Robin Wood and Polly Powell, of HarperCollins, for
giving me the opportunity to write it; to my agent Barbara Levy;
to the editorial team, especially Barbara Dixon and Jane Middleton;
to the design manager, Caroline Hill, and text designer, Joan Curtis;
to Dave Armstrong for the beautiful photographs, and not forgetting Simon Tutty
for all his help; to Lyn Rutherford for preparing the food so well for the
photographs; and to the stylist Róisín Nield. And special thanks to my husband
Robert, for his support and help in so many ways.

Text © Rose Elliot 1994
Photographs © David Armstrong 1994
All rights reserved under International and
Pan American Copyright Conventions.
Published in the United States by Random House, Inc., New York.

Published in Great Britain by
HarperCollins Publishers London in 1994.

Editor: *Jane Middleton*
Text designer: *Joan Curtis*
Photographer: *David Armstrong*
Home Economist: *Lyn Rutherford*
Stylist: *Róisín Nield*
Illustrator: *Lucinda Rogers*
Indexer: *Susan Bosanko*

For HarperCollins*Publishers*
Commissioning Editor: *Polly Powell*
Project Editor: *Barbara Dixon*
Design Manager: *Caroline Hill*

ISBN 0-679-76207-8

Typset in Palatino
Color reproductions by Amilcare Pizzi, S.p.A.
Printed and bound in Italy by Amilcare Pizzi S.p.A.

24689753

INTRODUCTION

✳

As the pace of life gets faster and faster there seems to be less and less time to cook. The range of fresh ingredients available, however, has never been greater, so the best way to cope is to make the most of these in order to produce good meals quickly without resorting to convenience foods. If you use really good ingredients that are naturally full of flavor, you don't have to do much to them in order to make a great meal. You just need a bit of know-how and a few simple recipes, which is what this book is all about. It's a collection of my favorite fast-food recipes, all taking about 30 minutes or less – some a lot less – to make, and they're all prepared from wholesome ingredients in as near-natural a state as possible. Many of the recipes are as quick to make as heating up a frozen meal or getting restaurant takeout, and they certainly taste better and do you more good. So good vegetarian food can be fast food – in fact it's what I make nearly all the time.

I've kept the recipes as simple as possible and arranged them under 'pantry' sections, so you can check what you've got in or what looks good in the store and then choose a recipe accordingly. Most of the recipes can be varied and you can often substitute one ingredient for another, so don't feel too restricted when you're following them.

I've also kept the range of equipment quite minimal, and all the recipes can be made on top of the stove or under the broiler – you don't need to use the oven so you won't have to wait for it to heat up. Many of the recipes serve just one or two people because this seems to be most appropriate for this kind of cooking, but you can always multiply the amounts if necessary. However many you're cooking for – one, two or a crowd – I hope you'll find this book helpful and inspiring and will enjoy making the recipes and eating good vegetarian fast food.

Rose Elliot

CONTENTS

BREAD

There's a huge range of delicious breads around now, and it's fun to try different types. In this section I've included some of my favorites – not just breads and rolls but also more unusual products such as poppadums, as well as croissants, bagels, panettone and brioche. Plenty of other interesting baked goods are worth experimenting with, and they all make an ideal basis for fast food. For a long time bread was unfairly dismissed as a filler, but now it is recognized as a healthy food which contributes valuable minerals and vitamins, as well as protein and energy, to diet.

EGGS, CHEESE & DAIRY FOODS

These foods are easy to turn into a quick feast, with dishes such as Spanish Omelet, Spinach and Stilton Crêpes, Haloumi with Spiced Leeks or Chocolate Amaretti Pie. Cheese is perfect for simple instant meals – see No-Cook Cheese Feasts for ideas – and yogurt, soft cheeses and cream form the basis of quick and easy desserts. Dairy products do contain fat, but used in moderation and balanced with vegetables, fruit and cereals they definitely have a place in a healthy, fast-food diet.

PASTA

As long as you have a packet of pasta in the cupboard you can always rustle up a quick meal: pasta is good even when served simply with just olive oil or butter. If you add a few more ingredients and make sure you have plenty of different pasta shapes in your storecupboard, the scope is enormous. Dishes such as Quick Mediterranean Pasta, Fusilli with Fennel and Snow Peas, Spinach Tagliatelle with Walnuts and Fettucine with Asparagus Sauce can all be made within 30 minutes, and they need little accompaniment – perhaps a simple salad or some bread – to make a satisfying meal.

LEGUMES, GRAINS & NUTS

LEGUMES, GRAINS & NUTS

These are packed full of nutrients. Nuts are a very concentrated source of energy, and small quantities go a long way. They make a wonderful fast food – great for putting into lunchboxes with some salad or fruit for a nourishing, fastest-ever meal. Most legumes need soaking and long cooking, so all the recipes in this book rely on canned ones to save time, except for red lentils which cook quickly without soaking. Grains are invaluable, too, and are much richer in protein, minerals and vitamins than many people realize.

VEGETABLES

VEGETABLES

Vegetables are excellent fast foods and make the basis of hundreds of speedy dishes. Most are quick to cook or can be served raw, and now that you can buy many of them ready washed the preparation time is even quicker. They can be made into wonderful main courses such as Provençal Potatoes, Broccoli with Cashew Sauce or Broiled Mediterranean Vegetables with Mozzarella; comforting soups, including Green Pea and Mint and Creamy Onion; or salads such as Thai Cabbage Salad or Italian Country Salad; vegetables are so versatile that there's plenty of scope for experiment.

FRUIT

FRUIT

If you're looking for something to give you a quick burst of energy, fruit beats sugary convenience foods any day; it's easy to carry, sweet and delicious to eat, and doesn't make you fat or rot your teeth. But fruit isn't just for snacking. It can also be the basis of appetizers, such as Three-Pear Salad, and light main courses, such as Apricots with Ricotta and Mint or Tarragon Pear with Cream Cheese. And, of course, fruit is perfect for quick nutritious desserts, from light, refreshing Peaches in Wine or Rhubarb and Ginger Compote to more substantial puddings such as Blueberry Crumble.

THE PANTRY

———————— ✳ ————————

Most of the recipes in this book are based on a combination of fresh ingredients and ingredients that keep well in a cupboard, such as pasta, rice and spices. A well-stocked pantry saves time; after the initial stocking-up it's just a matter of replenishing it when required. You don't have to shop every day to make quick vegetarian meals: fresh vegetables and dairy produce keep very well in the fridge; fresh herbs in jugs of water or growing in pots in a light place; and bread, if you want some in reserve, in the freezer. These are the ingredients I find most useful to have in stock, and many of the recipes in this book rely on them.

DRY GOODS

I like to keep in several packets of pasta in different shapes and a supply of split red lentils, which cook more quickly than other legumes and don't need soaking. Various types of rice are also indispensable: brown basmati is the only wholegrain rice that cooks in under 30 minutes, and white basmati takes even less time. Bulgur wheat, couscous, quick-cooking polenta, chick pea (gram) flour, cornstarch and dry breadcrumbs are worth having for occasional use, and flour (both white and whole wheat) and baking powder are cupboard basics. Graham crackers and amaretti cookies keep fairly well and make a good base for various desserts. Dried fruits are useful for both sweet and savory dishes, as are nuts, seeds and unsweetened, shredded coconut. Try to keep several types of nuts and seeds in stock, such as walnuts, hazelnuts, cashews, pine nuts, sunflower seeds and sesame seeds. If possible, store nuts in the fridge or freezer to prevent them from going rancid. In any case, it is best to buy them in small quantities.

CANNED AND FROZEN FOOD

Certain canned ingredients are invaluable for making fast food – chick peas, different types of beans, canned corn kernels (without added sugar), artichoke hearts and tomatoes in juice. Canned whole tomatoes are usually of better quality than the chopped ones and it's easy to break them up quickly with a spoon once they're in the saucepan. Canned chestnuts come in handy, whether it's to make a hearty winter stew or whip up a luxurious quick dessert. I like the vacuum-packed canned whole chestnuts that are now available. Frozen foods I like to keep in stock are corn kernels, peas and leaf spinach. Frozen heavy cream is useful, too, especially if you freeze it in ice-cube trays for when you need just a small quantity.

FLAVORING INGREDIENTS

Flavoring ingredients are doubly important for fast food, because you need to add interest and intensity of taste without a lengthy cooking period. It's worth spending a little time and money, therefore, building up a collection of spices and herbs, sweet and savory flavorings, and good oils and vinegars.

At the most basic level, you need good salt – I like flaky coarse sea salt which you can crush in your fingers – and a grinder for black peppercorns. Other basics are light olive oil for shallow-frying and a good-quality virgin olive oil for salad dressings. For stir-frying and occasional deep-frying I use peanut oil because it is the most stable at high temperatures; also dark sesame oil for adding flavor to stir-fries and oriental dishes. Vinegars to keep in stock are red wine vinegar, balsamic vinegar and light, sweet brown rice vinegar, all of which have their own individual character. Tabasco sauce and soy sauce pep up food instantly – choose soy sauce that is naturally matured and contains only soy beans and salt. Then there's mustard, preferably smooth Dijon as well as wholegrain mustard; good-quality store-bought mayonnaise; and jars of capers, black olive paste (the type made only with black olives and olive oil is best), sun-dried tomatoes, pesto sauce and black olives (my favorites are the Greek Kalamata or the little Niçois olives) – all of these are best kept in the fridge.

For sweet flavorings, I use both clear and thick honey and stem ginger preserved in syrup; I also find ginger jam useful. Rose and orange flower waters are versatile flavorings, and perhaps even better are liqueurs such as Cointreau or Amaretto, and eau de vie. My favorite is eau de vie de poire William – horribly expensive but divine in a delicate pear dessert.

The spices I find most useful are cinnamon (in sticks and ground), cloves, cardamom, cayenne, chili powder, whole and ground coriander, whole and ground cumin, ground turmeric, paprika, dried red chilies, and whole nutmegs for grating when needed. Mustard seeds and curry powder are good for occasional use. As far as herbs are concerned, thyme, sage, rosemary and oregano seem to survive the drying process well, and bay is actually better and more concentrated in flavor when dried. Being able to buy fresh herbs easily has made a huge difference to the fast cook's repertoire, and I find they all keep well in jars of water – fresh mint, basil, dill, cilantro, chives, chervil, tarragon and parsley (particularly Italian flat-leaf parsley) will liven up your cooking immensely. Lemon grass, green chilies and fresh ginger root are also widely available now, and are best kept in the fridge.

FRESH PRODUCE
Basic dairy produce such as eggs – from a reliable, salmonella-free source – milk, cream and yogurt should be kept in the fridge, along with soft and hard cheeses, including a block of fresh Parmesan for grating as required. Fresh vegetables such as tomatoes, salad leaves, carrots and cabbage keep well in the fridge, too. Other basic standbys are onions, garlic, potatoes, oranges and lemons, which I keep in a cool, dark cupboard, and bread, which goes into a bread bin, with a back-up supply in the freezer.

EQUIPMENT

The right equipment makes all the difference to the ease with which you can cook fast food. A little time spent removing clutter, re-thinking your needs, and streamlining and reorganizing kitchen surfaces and cupboards can save hours of your time over the weeks and months.

It's essential to invest in efficient kitchen tools. You don't need a lot of fancy equipment: the most important thing is a really good, sharp knife, and for that you do get what you pay for. Personally I like a classic Sabatier knife with a medium-length (4½-inch) blade. A good, solid chopping board is essential, too, the bigger the better. The other small tools I find indispensable are a swivel-bladed vegetable parer with a long handle that is really comfortable to hold, and a citrus zester, which is a curiously useful gadget. A garlic press is more bother than it is worth, in my opinion – you can do the job much more quickly and effectively with a knife and a board.

A food processor isn't essential, and many of the recipes in this book can be made without one, but it does open up many more possibilities – lovely creamy soups, quick pâtés and dips, for instance. As with so many things, if you're buying one it pays to get a larger version than you think you'll need; go for something simple in design which doesn't try to do too many jobs. Try to make a space for it on your work surface so that it's always there at the ready. An electric hand beater is also a surprisingly useful and labor-saving piece of equipment, and fairly inexpensive to buy. For years I put off buying one, and when eventually I did I couldn't believe how useful it was and wondered why I hadn't bought one earlier.

A microwave oven isn't essential by any means, and apart from a microwave version of risotto none of the recipes in this book depend on one. I find a crock-pot more useful than a microwave because I love making soups and it cooks them very quickly. Some people are wary of crock-pots because of all their hissing, but once you know what you are doing it can be invaluable.

Finally, a large saucepan with a steamer on top is helpful if you're cooking with limited space, because you can have one item cooking in the pan and a vegetable or something else steaming in the top. I have a stainless-steel steamer that I use a lot in this way.

BREAD

There's a huge range of delicious breads around now, and it's fun to try different types. In this section I've included some of my favorites – not just breads and rolls but also more unusual products such as poppadums, as well as croissants, bagels, panettone and brioche. Plenty of other interesting baked goods are worth experimenting with, and they all make an ideal basis for fast food. For a long time bread was unfairly dismissed as filler, but now it is recognized as a healthy food which contributes valuable minerals and vitamins, as well as protein and energy, to our diet.

CROSTINI & BRUSCHETTA
— ✳ —

These Italian toasts are really very similar: crostini are delicate rounds of light, crisp bread, whereas bruschetta is made from coarse country bread and rubbed with garlic to flavor it. They can be served plain to accompany soup, salads or dips, or topped with all kinds of delicious things to make canapés, quick snacks or light meals. If you are making a meal of them they are good served with some salad. You can use either a small or large baguette for crostini, depending on how big you want the rounds to be, and since one baguette yields about 50 slices, you only need a small piece to make a snack or meal for two people.

BASIC RECIPE

4 slices from a large baguette or 8 slices from a small one, cut ¼ inch thick, for crostini
2 slices from a country-style loaf for bruschetta

olive oil
1 garlic clove, peeled and cut in half, for bruschetta

1 Lay the slices of bread on a broiler pan and broil on both sides until they are dried out and slightly golden.
2 For crostini, brush the slices lightly with olive oil if you wish; I prefer them without. For bruschetta, rub the cut clove of garlic lightly over the surface and brush or drizzle with some olive oil. Serve plain, or with any of the toppings suggested below.
SERVES 2

TOPPINGS

All these toppings make enough for 8 small or 4 large crostini, or 2 bruschetta. Serve the crostini or bruschetta as soon as possible after adding the toppings.

— 1 —
CHERRY TOMATOES, FETA AND THYME

6–8 cherry tomatoes
crostini or bruschetta (see above)
¼ cup feta cheese

sprigs of thyme
freshly ground black pepper

1 Slice the cherry tomatoes and arrange them over the crostini or bruschetta, then crumble the feta cheese over them.
2 Snip a little fresh thyme over that and add a grinding of black pepper.

— 2 —
BLACK OLIVE PASTE, RED BELL PEPPER AND CAPERS

1 red bell pepper
black olive paste
crostini or bruschetta (see above)

2–3 tsp capers
a few leaves of flat-leaf parsley

1 Cut the bell pepper into quarters, then broil it for about 10 minutes or until the skin has blistered and charred in places.

2   Cool slightly, then remove the skin and seeds and slice or chop the flesh.

3   Spread black olive pâté over the crostini or bruschetta, then top with the red bell pepper, capers and a few leaves of flat-leaf parsley.

— 3 —

EGGPLANT AND MINT

1 medium eggplant	salt and freshly
olive oil	ground black pepper
4 sprigs of mint	crostini or bruschetta
balsamic vinegar	(see page 12)

1   Slice the eggplant into rounds about ⅛ inch thick and lay them on the broiler pan.

2   Brush with olive oil on both sides then broil on high for 5–10 minutes, until golden brown and tender.

3   Tear the mint sprigs and mix with the eggplant. Add a few drops of balsamic vinegar and salt and pepper to taste then divide between the crostini or bruschetta.

— 4 —

LENTILS WITH CRANBERRIES

This Christmassy variation can be made very quickly with canned lentils.

1 small onion, peeled and chopped	crostini or bruschetta (see page 12)
1 tbls olive oil	2 tbls cranberry sauce,
1¾ cups canned lentils	preferably containing whole cranberries
	sprigs of flat-leaf parsley

1   Fry the onion in the olive oil for 7–10 minutes, until soft and lightly browned.

2   Drain the lentils and add to the onion, mashing them a bit so that they hold together.

3   Spread this mixture on top of the crostini or bruschetta, piling it up well.

4   Dot the cranberry sauce over the top and decorate with sprigs of flat-leaf parsley.

— 5 —

BLUE CHEESE WITH GRAPES, PINE NUTS AND ENDIVE

crostini or bruschetta (see page 12)	4 ounces blue cheese 6 black grapes
a few endive leaves	a few pine nuts

1   Cover the crostini or bruschetta with endive leaves, breaking or shredding them as necessary.

2   Thinly slice the blue cheese and arrange on top.

3   Halve and seed the grapes and lay these on top, then scatter over a few pine nuts.

— 6 —

GOAT CHEESE, ARUGULA AND SUN-DRIED TOMATO

½ cup soft white goat cheese	several arugula leaves freshly ground black
crostini or bruschetta (see page 12)	pepper
8 sun-dried tomatoes in oil, drained	

1   Spread the soft white goat cheese thickly on the crostini or bruschetta.

2   Chop the sun-dried tomatoes and arrange them on top of the goat cheese, together with a few leaves of arugula, then grind some black pepper coarsely over the top.

— 7 —

HUMMUS, OLIVE AND PAPRIKA

½ cup hummus	olive oil
crostini or bruschetta (see page 12)	8 black olives a few sprigs of
paprika	flat-leaf parsley

1   Spread the hummus thickly on top of the crostini or bruschetta. Sprinkle some paprika over the top, then drizzle a little olive oil on top of that.

2   Decorate with the black olives and a sprig or two of flat-leaf parsley.

You can buy very good hummus at most of the big supermarkets and it makes an excellent topping for crostini.

BREAD

— 8 —
MUSHROOM PATE

2 cups mushrooms
2 tbs butter
1 garlic clove, crushed
2 eggs or 4 quail's eggs

salt and freshly
  ground black pepper
crostini or bruschetta
  (see page 12)
black olive paste

[1] Wash and dry the mushrooms then chop them
finely (use a food processor for this if you have
one). Melt the butter in a saucepan, put in the
mushrooms and garlic and cook them over a fairly
high heat until the mushrooms are tender and any
liquid they produce has evaporated – this may take
10 minutes.

[2] Meanwhile, boil the eggs for 10 minutes or the
quail's eggs for 2½ minutes. Peel them and slice
them fairly thinly, or cut the quail's eggs in half.
Season with salt and pepper.

[3] Season the mushroom mixture then either
leave it to cool slightly or spread it on the crostini or
bruschetta while still hot. Top with the egg slices
and a little black olive paste.

— 9 —
PLUM TOMATO, MOZZARELLA AND BASIL

Plum tomatoes usually have a good flavor and nice firm texture, but you could use other well-flavored tomatoes.

4 fresh plum tomatoes
salt and freshly
  ground black pepper
olive oil
2 ounces Mozzarella
  cheese (packed in
  water)

crostini or bruschetta
  (see page 12)
8 fresh basil leaves

[1] Slice the tomatoes into rounds, put them on a
plate and sprinkle them with salt, pepper and a few
drops of olive oil. Cut the Mozzarella cheese into
small pieces.

[2] Arrange the tomatoes on top of the crostini or
bruschetta then dot the cheese over the tomatoes.

[3] Tear the basil leaves over the top of the tomatoes and cheese and grind over some more black
pepper to taste.

— 10 —
GOLDY GREENY SPREAD

A strange and interesting recipe, adapted from New
Food For All Palates *by Sally and Lucian Berg
(Gollancz, 1967). Frozen beans are fine for this.*

1 onion, peeled and
  thinly sliced
2 tbs olive oil
4 ounces green beans
1 egg, hard-cooked

salt and freshly ground
  black pepper
crostini or bruschetta
  (see page 12)

[1] Fry the onion in the oil until golden brown and
crisp (this is very important for the flavor).

[2] Cook the green beans in a little boiling water
for 3–4 minutes, until tender, then drain.

[3] Peel and roughly chop the hard-cooked egg.
Put the beans, egg and half the onion into a food
processor and whizz to a purée. Season to taste.

[4] Spread on top of the crostini or bruschetta and
top with the remaining onion.

— 11 —
RICOTTA AND PEAR ON WATERCRESS

½ cup ricotta cheese
crostini or bruschetta
  (see page 12)
a little milk (optional)
a few watercress leaves
1 ripe pear

½ cup grated Parmesan
  cheese
freshly ground black
  pepper

[1] Spread the ricotta cheese over the crostini
or bruschetta (mix the cheese with a little milk first
if necessary).

[2] Press the watercress into the cheese. Peel, core
and thinly slice the pear and arrange on top.

[3] Sprinkle generously with the grated cheese
and grind some pepper over, then serve straight
away or flash under a hot broiler to melt the cheese.

OPPOSITE: *A selection of Crostini, topped with
Mushroom Pâté, Plum Tomato, Mozzarella and
Basil, and Goldy Greeny Spread*

QUICK PIZZAS
—— ✳ ——

*It's unrealistic to try and make a pizza from scratch in 30 minutes but you can make a
good quick tomato sauce, spread it over a ready-made base, add a topping and flash it under a
hot broiler. Although you can buy pizza bases, I like to use a range of different breads, such as
multigrain, ciabatta and English muffins. The bases and toppings in the following recipes can be
mixed and matched, if you prefer, to suit whatever ingredients you have to hand.*

TOMATO SAUCE

1 tbs olive oil
*1 onion, peeled and
  chopped*
2 garlic cloves, crushed
*1¼ cups canned
  tomatoes*

*8 sun-dried tomatoes
  in oil, drained
  (optional)*
*salt and freshly
  ground black pepper*

*To make a quick
lettuce salad, cut
a Bibb lettuce
across into thick
slices; wash and
drain in a colander,
then put into a
bowl, sprinkle with
1 tablespoon of
lemon juice, 2
2 tablespoons of
olive oil, some sea
salt and freshly
ground black pepper,
and toss lightly.*

1 Heat the oil in a saucepan, add the onion then
cover and cook gently for 10 minutes, until tender
but not brown.
2 Stir the garlic into the onion, cook for 1–2 minutes longer, then stir in the tomatoes, together with
their juice, breaking them up with a wooden spoon.
Chop the sun-dried tomatoes roughly, if you are
using them, and add these to the pan too.
3 Let the mixture simmer away for about 10–15
minutes until the liquid has evaporated. Season
with salt and pepper to taste.
MAKES ENOUGH FOR 2 ENGLISH MUFFINS, OR 1
MULTIGRAIN OR CIABATTA PIZZA

MUSHROOM PIZZA

*2 cups small white
  mushrooms*
2 tbs olive oil
*salt and freshly
  ground black pepper*
2 English muffins

*4 ounces Cheddar or
  other cheese*
*tomato sauce (see
  above)*

1 Wash and slice the mushrooms then fry them
in the olive oil for 1–2 minutes until they are tender.
Season with salt and pepper.
2 Cut the muffins in half and toast on both sides.
Thinly slice the cheese.
3 Heat the tomato sauce then spread it over the
muffins. Top with the mushrooms and cheese and
heat under the broiler for a few minutes, until the
pizzas are piping hot and the cheese is golden
brown and bubbling.
SERVES 2

RED AND YELLOW
PEPPER PIZZA

1 red bell pepper
1 yellow bell pepper
*1 oval or round
  multigrain loaf
  (14 ounces)*
olive oil
*tomato sauce (see
  above)*

*salt and freshly
  ground black pepper*
*⅔ cup grated
  Parmesan cheese*
*a few fresh basil
  leaves*

1 Cut the bell peppers into quarters, put them
cut-side down on a broiler pan and broil for about
10 minutes or until the skin has blistered and
charred in places. Remove from the broiler and,
when cool enough to handle, peel off the skin,
remove the seeds and stalk, and slice the peppers.
2 Cut the loaf horizontally in half, scoop out a

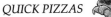

little of the crumb, then brush the inside with olive oil and toast it under the broiler. Toast both sides if you want a crisp pizza base.

③ Heat the tomato sauce then spread this evenly over the bread and top with the bell peppers, mixing up the colors. Season the peppers lightly, then sprinkle the grated cheese over the pizzas.

④ Heat the pizzas under the broiler for a few minutes until they are piping hot and the cheese is melted and lightly browned. Tear a little basil over the top and serve.

SERVES 2–4

CIABATTA PIZZA WITH ARTICHOKES

The nicest artichoke hearts to use for this are the ones that you can buy preserved in oil. Any that are left over keep well in the fridge. Alternatively, drained canned artichoke hearts make a good substitute.

1 red onion, peeled and sliced	tomato sauce (see opposite)
olive oil	4 ounces Mozzarella cheese
1 ciabatta loaf, or other Italian-style bread	1 cup sliced artichoke hearts

① Fry the onion in 1 tablespoon of olive oil until softened, about 5–7 minutes.

② Meanwhile, cut the loaf horizontally in half, brush each cut surface with olive oil and toast it under the broiler. Toast both sides if you want a crisp pizza base.

③ Heat the tomato sauce then spread it evenly over the bread. Slice the cheese and arrange it on top of the sauce, then top with the artichoke hearts and fried onion.

④ Heat the pizzas under the broiler for a few minutes until they are piping hot and the cheese is melted and lightly browned.

SERVES 2–4

GORGONZOLA AND WALNUT PIZZA

1 oval or round multigrain loaf (14 ounces)	4 ounces Gorgonzola cheese
olive oil	½ cup walnut pieces
tomato sauce (see opposite)	

① Cut the multigrain loaf horizontally in half, scoop out a little of the crumb, then brush the inside with olive oil and and toast it under the broiler. Toast both sides if you want a crisp pizza base.

② Heat the tomato sauce then spread this evenly over the bread. Slice the cheese and arrange it on top of the sauce, then top with the walnuts.

③ Heat the pizzas under the broiler for a few minutes until they are piping hot and the cheese is melted and lightly browned.

SERVES 2–4

PESTO PIZZA

1 ciabatta loaf, or other Italian-style bread	3 ounces Parmesan cheese
olive oil	2–4 tbs pesto sauce
tomato sauce (see opposite)	a few black olives (optional)

① Cut the loaf horizontally in half, brush each cut surface with olive oil and toast it under the broiler. Toast both sides if you want a crisp pizza base.

② Heat the tomato sauce then spread it over the bread. Slice the cheese into thin slivers and arrange on top of the sauce, then drizzle the pesto over everything and add the olives if you're using these.

③ Heat the pizzas under the broiler for a few minutes until they are piping hot and the cheese is melted and lightly browned.

SERVES 2–4

Ciabatta is an open-textured, oval shaped bread made with olive oil. If you can't find it substitute focaccia.

Bottled pesto is readily available nowadays, and some Italian delicatessens and large supermarkets stock fresh pesto sauce. If you have time, you might like to make your own (see page 59).

TWO-CHEESE PIZZA

2 English muffins
4 ounces Mozzarella
  cheese
2 ounces Parmesan
  cheese

12 black olives
tomato sauce (see
  page 16)

*Light rolls or
pieces of baguette
or focaccia bread,
split in half, also
make good bases
for these toppings.*

1. Cut the English muffins in half and toast them on both sides.
2. Meanwhile, thinly slice the cheeses and halve and pit the olives.
3. Heat the tomato sauce and spread it over the muffins, then top with the slices of cheese and the olives.
4. Heat the pizzas under the broiler for a few minutes until they are piping hot and the cheese is golden brown and bubbling.
SERVES 2

CORN AND CHERRY TOMATO PIZZA

2 English muffins
4 ounces Cheddar
  cheese
6 cherry tomatoes
tomato sauce (see
  page 16)

⅓ cup canned or frozen
  corn
  kernels
salt and freshly
  ground black pepper

1. Cut the English muffins in half and toast them on both sides.
2. Meanwhile, grate the cheese and slice the cherry tomatoes.
3. Heat the tomato sauce and spread it evenly over the muffins, then top with the grated cheese, corn kernels and cherry tomatoes. Season with salt and pepper.
4. Heat the pizzas under the broiler for a few minutes until they are piping hot and the cheese is golden brown and bubbling.
SERVES 2

RED BELL PEPPER, EGGPLANT AND GOAT CHEESE PIZZA

1 small red bell pepper
1 medium eggplant
olive oil
2 English muffins
tomato sauce (see
  page 16)

salt and freshly
  ground black pepper
2 ounces firm goat
  cheese

1. Cut the bell pepper into quarters then put it cut-side down on a broiler pan. Cut the eggplant into slices about ⅛ inch thick and lay these on the broiler pan too. Brush the eggplant slices on both sides with olive oil then broil on high for 5–10 minutes, until the skin on the pepper is blistered and charred in places and the eggplant is golden brown and tender. Remove from the broiler but leave it on. Cover the pepper with a damp cloth.
2. Cut the English muffins in half and toast them on both sides.
3. Heat the tomato sauce then spread it over the muffins and top with the eggplant slices. Remove the loose skin and seeds from the bell pepper, cut it into long, thin strips and arrange on top of the eggplant. Season with salt and pepper.
4. Break off small pieces of goat cheese and dot them over the top of the pizzas. Grind a little black pepper coarsely over the goat cheese then heat the pizzas under the broiler for a few minutes until they are piping hot.
SERVES 2

OPPOSITE: *Two-Cheese Pizza, Corn and Cherry Tomato Pizza, Red Bell Pepper, Eggplant and Goat Cheese Pizza*

SNACKS ON TOAST
———— * ————

TOASTED CHEESE

This simple version of cheese on toast is quick and easy to make and you can vary it by using different types of bread and cheese, substituting beer, wine or apple cider for the milk, and adding extra ingredients such as tomatoes, onion, herbs, mushrooms, chutney or pickles – whatever takes your fancy.

1–2 slices of bread
¾–1 cup grated
  Cheddar cheese
1–2 tbs milk

freshly ground black
  pepper

1   Preheat the broiler and toast the bread on one side.

2   Mix the cheese with the milk to make a paste then season with freshly ground black pepper.

3   Spread the cheese mixture on the untoasted side of the bread, broil until puffed up and golden brown then serve at once.
SERVES 1

VARIATIONS

1 WITH ASPARAGUS

This is an extremely nice variation if you are making toasted cheese for more than one person and want something that is extra special. Allow about 3–4 asparagus spears per person, trim them then cut them into 1-inch lengths and cook in boiling water for 2–4 minutes, until just tender. Drain and serve heaped on top of the toasted cheese.

2 WITH APPLE CIDER AND APPLES

Use apple cider instead of the milk. Peel and core a small, mellow dessert apple, then cut it into thin rings or slices and arrange it on the toast. Cover with the cheese mixture and place under the broiler until the cheese is puffed up and golden brown and the apple is tender.

3 WITH OLIVES

I like this best made with feta cheese, which you can crumble rather than grate. Add 6–8 black or green olives, or a mixture of both, to the cheese.

4 WITH ONION AND MUSTARD

Mix the cheese with beer instead of milk and add ½–1 teaspoon of mustard and 1 finely chopped small onion.

5 WITH CHILI

De-seed and finely chop 1 small green chili and add it to the grated cheese.

MOZZARELLA IN CARROZZA

Use the best Mozzarella you can find – certainly one packed in water – for this delicious mixture of hot melting cheese and crisp fried bread.

4 ounces Mozzarella
  cheese
4 slices of bread, crusts
  removed

2 eggs
olive oil

1   Drain and slice the cheese and sandwich it between the slices of bread, pressing them firmly together.

2   Lightly beat the eggs, then strain them into a shallow dish. Put the sandwiches in the egg and leave them for a few minutes to soak it up, turning them over once.

3   Heat a little olive oil in a skillet and fry the sandwiches on both sides until they are golden brown and crisp. Drain them quickly on paper towels and serve at once.
SERVES 2

Mozzarella in Carrozza means 'Mozzarella in a carriage', a poetic and apt description.

BUTTERY SCRAMBLED EGGS ON TOAST

2 slices of bread
butter
4 eggs

salt and freshly
ground black pepper

1   Toast the bread, butter it and keep it warm.
2   Lightly beat the eggs and season with salt and pepper.
3   Melt a little butter in a saucepan. When it sizzles, add the eggs and cook over a low heat for a few minutes, stirring.
4   Just before the eggs set, move the pan from the heat and, to make the scrambled eggs extra delicious, stir in a few slivers of butter. The eggs will continue to cook in the heat of the pan.
5   Pile the scrambled eggs on to the toast and serve at once on warmed plates.

SERVES 2

VARIATIONS

1 WITH FRESH HERBS

Add 1–2 tablespoons of chopped fresh herbs at the end of the cooking time, along with the extra butter.

2 PIPERADE

Piperade takes longer to cook than plain scrambled eggs but it is nice when you want something a bit more substantial.

Melt 2 tablespoons of butter in a pan then add 1 large onion, peeled and chopped, and 1 green bell pepper, de-seeded and chopped. Cover and cook for 10 minutes, until soft but not browned, then add 1 pound of tomatoes, peeled and chopped, and 1 clove of garlic, crushed. Cook gently, uncovered, for about 10 minutes, until the vegetables are soft but not mushy. Meanwhile, toast and butter 4 slices of multigrain or whole wheat bread, cut it into fingers and keep it warm. Lightly beat 4 eggs then pour them into the pan with the vegetables and stir gently until they begin to set. Remove from the heat (the eggs will continue to cook in the heat of the pan), season and serve immediately with the toast fingers.

CLUB SANDWICH

3 slices of whole
  wheat bread
butter
2 lettuce leaves
1 small tomato, sliced
mayonnaise or
  mustard

½ small avocado
salt and freshly
  ground black pepper
4 wooden toothpicks
4 stuffed olives

1   Toast the bread, butter one piece and arrange the lettuce, tomato and a little mayonnaise or mustard on top.
2   Cover with another piece of toast, buttered on both sides. Peel, pit and slice the avocado, arrange on top of the toast and season with salt and pepper.
3   Butter the third piece of toast and place, butter-side down, on top of the avocado. Press down on the sandwich, cut it into quarters then spear each quarter with a wooden toothpick and decorate with a stuffed olive.

SERVES 1

CAMEMBERT TOAST WITH APRICOT PRESERVES

I love the combination of Camembert cheese and something sweet. If you find the preserves too sweet, however, mango chutney is also very good.

1 slice of whole wheat
  bread
2 portions of
  Camembert cheese

2–3 tsp good-quality
  apricot preserves
2–3 tsp chopped
  hazelnuts

1   Heat the broiler. Toast the bread on both sides.
2   Mash the Camembert roughly on the toast then put some dollops of apricot preserves on top of that.
3   Broil until the cheese has melted then sprinkle with the nuts and broil again until lightly browned.

SERVES 1

A good way of using up the other half of the avocado is to make guacamole; mash the avocado with 1 peeled, chopped tomato and some finely chopped chili; then add plenty of chopped fresh cilantro and season to taste.

OPEN SANDWICHES & PAN BAGNAT

RADICCHIO AND CREAM CHEESE

⅓ cup cream cheese or
  farmer's cheese
2 slices of dark rye
  bread
a few radicchio leaves

2 dill pickles, sliced
sprigs of fresh dill
  (optional)

1 Spread about half of the cream cheese or farmer's cheese on the bread, then press the radicchio leaves on top of that.

2 Spoon the remaining cheese on top, then arrange slices of dill pickle on top of that and finish with a sprig of fresh dill, if you like.

SERVES 2

EGG AND OLIVE

2 slices of white
  poppyseed bread
mayonnaise
4 curly endive leaves

1 hard-cooked egg
6 black olives
paprika

1 Spread the bread with a thin layer of mayonnaise then arrange the curly endive on top.

2 Chop the hard-cooked egg into chunks and mix with a little mayonnaise to moisten. Divide this mixture between the bread slices and garnish with the olives and a little paprika.

SERVES 2

BRIE AND RED ONION

mayonnaise
2 slices of whole wheat
  bread
2–4 Bibb lettuce leaves
2 ounces Brie

3–4 slices of red onion
a few walnuts

1 Spread a thin layer of mayonnaise on the bread then arrange the lettuce on top, pressing it down into the mayonnaise to make it stick.

2 Slice the Brie thinly, then arrange it on top of the lettuce with the red onion slices and sprinkle with a few walnuts.

SERVES 2

PAN BAGNAT

1 long baguette
1 pound tomatoes
salt and freshly ground
  black pepper
1 lettuce

8 ounces Mozzarella
  cheese
1 large avocado
lemon juice
fresh basil leaves

1 Cut the baguette into quarters. Slice each piece open and scoop out most of the crumb.

2 Slice the tomatoes and sprinkle with salt. Wash the lettuce and spin or pat dry; slice the Mozzarella cheese; pit, peel and slice the avocado and sprinkle the slices with lemon juice, salt and pepper.

3 Fill the bread with layers of the ingredients, adding torn basil leaves and seasoning to each layer. If you are eating the sandwiches later, wrap them tightly and keep in the fridge until needed.

SERVES 4

OPPOSITE: *(top) Pan Bagnat and (bottom) Open Sandwiches*

You can vary the filling for pan bagnat according to your taste and what is available: try adding slices of cheese, or cream cheese, hummus with some olives, or any of the fillings given for pita pockets (see pages 24–5). The main thing is to be generous with the filling.

22

PITA POCKETS

—— * ——

Pita breads make very convenient containers for all kinds of delicious ingredients that would be too moist or bulky to put in a sandwich. Salads and stir-fries can be piled into warmed pita pockets; grilled vegetables, too, freshly cooked and still sizzling; and simple mixtures of beans, vegetables, cheese and hummus. Here is a selection of fillings.

You can sprinkle the eggplant with salt, leave it for 30 minutes, then rinse it if you wish; this isn't usually necessary as a precaution against bitterness, but it can reduce the amount of oil the eggplant absorbs.

SPICED CHICK PEAS

A tomato, sliced into quarters or eighths, is nice added to this for a change.

1 onion, peeled and
  finely chopped
2 tbs olive oil
2 garlic cloves, crushed
1 tsp cumin seeds
1¾ cups canned chick
  peas, drained
2 pita breads

4–6 lettuce leaves
4 tbs thick creamy
  yogurt, or a mixture
  of yogurt and good-
  quality mayonnaise
salt and freshly ground
  black pepper
paprika

1 Fry the onion in the oil, with a lid on the pan, for 5 minutes. Stir in the garlic and cumin seeds, cover again and cook for a further 2–3 minutes until the onion is tender.
2 Add the chick peas to the onion and cook for 4–5 minutes, until heated through and perhaps lightly browned in places.
3 Warm the pita breads under the broiler, then cut them lengthwise in half. Gently open up each half and put in the lettuce, tearing it as necessary, then spoon in the chick pea mixture. Season the yogurt or yogurt and mayonnaise, spoon on top of the chick peas and sprinkle with a little paprika. Serve at once.
SERVES 2

EGGPLANT WITH PESTO

1 large eggplant
olive oil
2 pita breads
1–2 tbs good-quality
  bought pesto sauce,
  or home-made (see
  page 59)

salt and freshly ground
  black pepper

1 Heat the broiler. Cut the eggplant lengthwise into slices about ⅛ inch thick and lay these on a broiler pan. Brush the slices on both sides with olive oil then broil on high for 5–10 minutes, turning them over as necessary, until golden brown and tender.
2 Warm the pita breads under the broiler, then cut them lengthwise in half and gently open up each half. Mix the eggplant slices with pesto to taste, season, then spoon them into the pita breads and serve at once.
SERVES 2

GREEK SALAD

4–6 lettuce leaves
small piece of
  cucumber
2 small tomatoes
4 scallions
a few black olives,
  pitted
2 tbs olive oil

2 tsp wine vinegar
salt and freshly
  ground black pepper
4 ounces feta cheese
chopped fresh mint or
  oregano
2 pita breads

1 Wash the salad ingredients then tear the lettuce, dice the cucumber, slice the tomatoes, chop the scallions and put them into a bowl. Add the olives, oil, vinegar and a grinding of pepper.

2 Cut the feta into cubes and mix it with the other ingredients, then add the fresh mint or oregano and a little salt if necessary.

3 Warm the pita breads through under the broiler, then cut them lengthwise in half, gently open up each half and fill with the feta mixture.
SERVES 2

COUSCOUS, TOMATO AND MINT

⅔ *cup couscous*	*juice of 1 lemon*
⅓ *cup raisins*	*4 tbs chopped fresh*
(optional)	*mint*
2 scallions	*salt and freshly ground*
4 tomatoes	*black pepper*
2 pita breads	

1 Put the couscous and the raisins, if you are using them, into a bowl and cover with boiling water. Leave on one side for 10 minutes.

2 Meanwhile, trim and chop the scallions, chop the tomatoes and warm the pita breads under the broiler.

3 Drain the couscous and mix with the scallions, tomatoes, lemon juice, mint and salt and pepper to taste.

4 Split the pita breads lengthwise in half, gently open each half and fill with the couscous mixture.
SERVES 2

RED BEAN AND CORN

2 tbs olive oil	*1 cup canned corn*
1 small onion, peeled	*kernels*
and chopped	*1 cup canned red*
1 small green bell	*kidney beans,*
pepper, chopped	*drained*
¾ *cup canned*	*salt and freshly*
tomatoes	*ground black pepper*
	2 pita breads

1 Heat the oil in a pan, put in the onion and bell pepper, cover and cook gently for 10 minutes, or until they are getting tender.

2 Mash in the tomatoes with their juice, cover and cook for a further 10 minutes, then add the corn and kidney beans. Cook gently for a few more minutes until hot. Season with salt and pepper.

3 Warm the pita breads under the broiler, then cut them lengthwise in half, gently open up each half, fill with the red bean mixture and serve at once.
SERVES 2

CHEESE AND CARROT VINAIGRETTE

2 carrots (about	*2 tbs olive oil*
8 ounces)	*2 tsp wine vinegar*
4 ounces Cheddar	*salt and freshly ground*
cheese	*black pepper*
4 scallions	*2 pita breads*

1 Scrape or peel the carrots then coarsely grate the carrots and cheese into a bowl. Trim and slice the scallions and add them to the bowl, together with the oil, vinegar and a seasoning of salt and pepper. Mix well.

2 Warm the pita breads under the broiler, then cut them lengthwise in half, gently open up each half, fill with the carrot mixture and serve at once.
SERVES 2

You could use bulgur wheat instead of couscous for a change: prepare it in the same way.

25

TORTILLAS & POPPADUMS

TORTILLA SALAD ROLLS

2 tortillas
6–8 iceberg lettuce
  leaves
2 tomatoes
small piece of
  cucumber
2 scallions

4 tbs mayonnaise, sour
  cream, yogurt or a
  mixture
hot chili sauce such as
  Tabasco
salt and freshly
  ground black pepper

1 Put the tortillas into a skillet over a moderate heat, one at a time, to warm through, or heat them under the broiler.

2 Shred the lettuce leaves and chop the tomatoes, cucumber and scallions quite finely. Mix with the mayonnaise, sour cream or yogurt then add a dash of hot chili sauce and some salt and pepper to taste.

3 Spread the salad mixture on to the warm tortillas, roll them up firmly and serve at once.
SERVES 2

POPPADUMS WITH AVOCADO AND CURRIED MAYONNAISE

2 tsp curry powder
2 tbs mayonnaise
2 tbs plain yogurt
1 tsp mango chutney
salt and freshly
  ground black pepper

1 avocado
2 tomatoes
squeeze of lemon juice
2–3 poppadums
paprika pepper or
  fresh cilantro leaves

OPPOSITE: *(left) Pita Pockets with (top) Cheese and Carrot Vinaigrette and (bottom) Red Bean and Corn, page 25, and (right) Poppadums with Avocado and Curried Mayonnaise*

1 Put the curry powder into a dry saucepan and heat for 1–2 minutes until it smells aromatic. Remove from the heat and mix with the mayonnaise, yogurt, chutney and salt and pepper to taste.

2 Peel, pit and chop the avocado then put it in a bowl. Dice the tomatoes and add to the avocado with the lemon juice and salt and pepper to taste.

3 Put the poppadums on a plate, spoon the avocado mixture on the side and trickle the curried mayonnaise over it. Finish with a sprinkling of paprika pepper or a little chopped fresh cilantro.
SERVES 1

RED BEAN BURRITOS

2 onions, peeled and
  chopped
2 tbs olive oil
2 garlic cloves, crushed
1 chili, de-seeded and
  chopped
1 tsp cumin seeds
2 tomatoes

1¾ cups canned red
  kidney beans, drained
2 tbs chopped fresh
  cilantro
salt and freshly ground
  black pepper
2 tortillas
sour cream to serve

1 Fry the onions in the oil, with a lid on the pan, for 5 minutes. Add the garlic, chili and cumin and cook for 1–2 minutes.

2 Cover the tomatoes with boiling water for a few seconds, then drain and slip off the skins. Chop and add to the pan with the kidney beans. Cook gently for 5 minutes or until heated through, mashing the beans to make a rough purée. Add the cilantro and season with salt and pepper.

3 Warm the tortillas one at a time in a skillet over a moderate heat, or heat them under the broiler. Spread the bean mixture on the warm tortillas, roll them up and serve with sour cream.
SERVES 2

Poppadums are very thin and brittle Indian flatbreads. They are available from Indian food stores and some large delis.

27

CROISSANTS, ROLLS & SWEET IDEAS

---- ✳ ----

SPEEDY GARLIC BREAD

Although garlic bread is usually made in the oven, you can speed things up by using the broiler instead.

½ *baguette or 2 French*   *4 tbs softened*
  bread rolls, white or   *butter*
  whole wheat
2 garlic cloves, crushed

1   Heat the broiler. Cut the baguette on the diagonal into slices about 1 inch thick, or cut the rolls in half.
2   Mix together the garlic and butter then spread this over the cut surfaces of the bread.
3   Broil the bread until hot and sizzling, then turn it over to heat the other side. Serve immediately, or cover with aluminum foil and keep warm.
SERVES 2

CREAMY ASPARAGUS CROISSANTS

This delicious snack is rather like a cheat's version of feuilleté of asparagus in cream.

4 – 8 ounces asparagus   *salt and freshly ground*
  spears   *black pepper*
1 tbs butter   *freshly grated nutmeg*
1½ tsp cornstarch   *2 croissants*
⅔ *cup light*
  cream

1   Trim the asparagus as necessary and cut it into 1-inch lengths. Keep the tips separate from the stems.
2   Cook the chopped stems in 1 inch of boiling water for 2 minutes, then add the tips and cook for

Cheese and Garlic Bread makes a nice variation: simply put slivers of cheese (such as Gruyère) on the garlic bread before broiling it; or try herb bread, using 1 tablespoon of chopped fresh parsley and chives instead of, or as well as, the garlic.

a further 2 minutes, until they are beginning to get tender but are still crunchy. Drain.
3   Melt the butter in a pan and stir in the cornstarch. Add the cream and stir over a moderate heat until it comes to the boil and thickens. Cook for 1–2 minutes then remove from the heat and stir in the asparagus. Season with salt, pepper and nutmeg.
4   Slice the croissant horizontally in half. Toast on both sides until crisp and lightly browned.
5   Serve the croissant halves with the asparagus, sandwiching them together with the mixture if you like, and letting the excess run on to the plate.
SERVES 2

GARLIC MUSHROOM ROLL

1½ cups small white   *salt and freshly*
  mushrooms   *ground black pepper*
1 tbs butter   *1 high, rounded*
1 tsp olive oil   *sourdough or French*
1–2 garlic cloves,   *bread roll*
  crushed

1   Wash and roughly chop the mushrooms, then fry them in the butter and olive oil for 5 minutes or until they are tender. If they give off a lot of liquid, go on cooking them until this has evaporated; this may take as long as 10 minutes.
2   Add the garlic and cook for 1–2 minutes longer. Season with salt and pepper.
3   Meanwhile, heat the broiler. Slice the top off the roll to make a lid; scoop out and discard most of the crumb. Warm through the roll and lid under the broiler, turning it.
4   Spoon the mushrooms into the roll and replace the lid. Serve at once.
SERVES 1

CHUTNEY BEAN BURGER

Use whatever chutney or pickles you like in this; you could also add extras such as grated cheese, mustard, mayonnaise, sliced tomato and lettuce to make a kind of burger with everything.

1 onion, peeled and chopped
1 tbs olive oil
1 garlic clove, crushed
1 cup canned butter beans, drained

1–2 tbs chutney or pickles
salt and freshly ground black pepper
1 soft burger roll

1 Fry the onion in the olive oil, with a lid on the pan, for 5 minutes. Add the garlic to the pan and cook for 1–2 minutes longer.
2 Add the beans to the pan and cook gently for about 5 minutes, until heated through, mashing the beans to make a rough purée. Stir in the chutney or pickles and season with salt and pepper.
3 Heat the broiler. Cut the burger roll in half and warm it through under the broiler, then pile the bean mixture on one half, top with the other half, press down and serve immediately.
SERVES 1

BRIOCHE WITH TRIPLE CREME AND APRICOT CONSERVE

An indulgent breakfast, brunch or dessert.

1 individual brioche
4 ounces Triple Crème cheese

1–2 tbs best-quality apricot conserve

1 Warm the brioche in the oven or under the broiler, then serve with the Triple Crème cheese and apricot conserve.
SERVES 1

GINGER AND CREAM CHEESE BAGELS

½ cup cream cheese, low fat or regular
2 pieces of preserved stem ginger
6 walnut halves

a little milk (optional)
2 bagels

1 Put the cream cheese into a bowl. Finely chop the ginger and walnuts and beat them into the cream cheese, adding a little milk if necessary to soften it.
2 Cut the bagels in half, spread with the filling and sandwich together.
SERVES 2

BAGELS WITH CHOPPED-HERRING-WITHOUT-HERRING

This filling is a piquant and intriguing relish from New Food For All Palates *by Sally and Lucian Berg. It also makes a good topping for crostini or bruschetta.*

1 slice of white bread, crusts removed
7 tsp white wine vinegar
2 eggs, hard-cooked
¼ onion

¼ green bell pepper
¼ tart apple, peeled
1 rounded tsp sea salt
4 tsp olive oil
white pepper
2 bagels

1 Tear the bread into pieces, put these into a bowl and sprinkle with the vinegar.
2 Peel the eggs, chop them roughly and put them into a food processor with the onion, green bell pepper and apple, also in rough chunks. Add the bread, salt and oil and whizz to a chunky purée. Season, adding some white pepper to taste.
3 Cut the bagels in half, spread the filling over them and sandwich together.
SERVES 2

Panettone is a yeasted Italian festive bread, usually containing dried fruit.

PANETTONE WITH FRESH FIGS

This makes a good quick festive dessert. Other fruits such as clementines, peeled and sliced, could be substituted for the figs, or instead of the fresh fruit you could use fruits preserved in alcohol.

6–8 fresh figs
4 slices of panettone
1 cup thick creamy yogurt

a few slivered almonds

1. Wash and slice the figs, then arrange them on individual plates with a slice of panettone, a good dollop of thick yogurt and a few slivered almonds.
SERVES 4

CINNAMON TOAST WITH HONEYED APPLES

Rather like an apple charlotte, this is a pleasant combination of crisp, sugary cinnamon toast and buttery apple slices. The recipe also works well with pears instead of apples, and white bread rather than brown. Some chilled thick yogurt or light cream makes a good accompaniment.

2 sweet, mellow dessert apples
butter
2 tbs honey
2–4 slices of whole-wheat bread

2–4 tbs raw cane or brown sugar
ground cinnamon

1. Peel the apples, cut them into quarters, remove the cores, then cut each quarter into thin slices.
2. Heat a little butter in a saucepan and add the apples and honey. Cook, uncovered, over a gentle heat, until the apple slices have softened, about 3–4 minutes, stirring gently from time to time.

3. Meanwhile, make the cinnamon toast: toast the bread on both sides – don't get it too brown and crisp. Remove the crusts if you like, then butter the toast. Cover each slice evenly with sugar and sprinkle with cinnamon.
4. Put the toast under the broiler for 1–2 minutes until the sugar has melted a bit to make a crisp coating. Cut into fingers or triangles.
5. Spoon the apple slices on to a small plate and arrange the cinnamon toast around them.
SERVES 2

CROISSANT WITH CREAM AND BLACK CHERRY CONSERVE

Unless a croissant is superb in flavor and texture, I think that halving and toasting it is by far the nicest way to serve it – either with butter or with a sweet or savory filling. Here, a combination of three of my favorite foods makes an indulgent occasional treat.

1 croissant
1–2 tbs black cherry conserve
1–2 tbs thick heavy cream, crème fraîche or sour cream

a little confectioners' sugar (optional)

1. Slice the croissant in half horizontally. Toast on both sides until crisp and lightly browned.
2. Spread the bottom half with black cherry conserve, cover with the cream, then replace the top half of the croissant.
3. Sift a little confectioners' sugar over, if you like.
SERVES 1

OPPOSITE: *(left) Panettone with Fresh Figs, (top) Croissant with Cream and Black Cherry Conserve, (right) Cinnamon Toast with Honeyed Apples*

EGGS, CHEESE & DAIRY FOODS

These foods are easy to turn into a quick feast, with dishes such as Spanish Omelet, Spinach and Stilton Crêpes, Haloumi with Spiced Leeks or Chocolate Amaretti Pie. Cheese is perfect for simple instant meals – see No-Cook Cheese Feasts for ideas – and yogurt, soft cheeses and cream form the basis of quick and easy desserts. Dairy products do contain fat, but used in moderation and balanced with vegetables, fruit and cereals they definitely have a place in a healthy, fast-food diet.

OMELETS
———— ✳ ————

SUN-DRIED TOMATO AND HERB OMELET

2 eggs
4 sun-dried tomatoes
  in oil, drained
2 tbls chopped fresh
  herbs, such as chervil,
  chives and parsley

salt and freshly
  ground black pepper
1 tbs butter

If you are making a sweet soufflé omelet, for a flashy finish fill the omelet with your chosen mixture, fold it in half, then sift 2 tablespoons of confectioners' sugar over the top and caramelize the sugar by laying a red-hot skewer on top for a moment or two in a criss-cross pattern.

1 Break the eggs into a bowl and beat them lightly until just combined. Chop the sun-dried tomatoes and add to the eggs, together with the herbs. Season with salt and pepper.
2 Put a 6-inch skillet over a medium heat. When it is hot add the butter, turn the heat up and swirl the butter around – don't let it brown.
3 Pour in the eggs, tilting the skillet to distribute them evenly, then, using a fork, draw the set edges towards the center and let the liquid egg run to the edges. Repeat until the omelet is almost set.
4 Tilt the skillet over a warmed plate, then fold the edge of the omelet over to the center and let it fold over again on to the plate. Serve immediately.
SERVES 1

VARIATIONS

1 CHEESE AND HERB

Add 1½ tablespoons of grated Gruyère cheese to the beaten eggs instead of the tomatoes. When the omelet is almost set, sprinkle another 1½ tablespoons of grated cheese over the center.

2 FRESH TOMATO

Peel, de-seed and chop 1 large tomato, warm it through in a little butter in a small pan and season. When the omelet is almost set, spoon the tomato over the center. You could add some chopped scallions, or some fresh basil or other herbs, too, if you like. Turn out the omelet and serve dusted with finely grated fresh Parmesan cheese.

SOUFFLE OMELET

Halfway between a soufflé and an omelet (though far quicker to cook than a soufflé) a soufflé omelet makes a pleasant change and can be served with sweet or savory fillings.

2 eggs, separated
salt and freshly
  ground black pepper
  (for a savory
  omelet)

1 tbs butter

1 Heat the broiler. Put the egg yolks into a bowl, add 2 tablespoons of water, and some seasoning if you're making a savory omelet, and mix well.
2 Whisk the egg whites until they stand in stiff peaks, but don't let them get too dry. Stir a spoonful of beaten egg white into the yolks, then gently fold in the rest with a metal spoon.
3 Heat a 6-inch skillet over a moderate heat then put in the butter and tilt the skillet so that the butter coats the sides. Pour the egg mixture into the skillet and cook over a moderate heat for 1–2 minutes, until golden brown underneath. Put the skillet under the broiler for 1–2 minutes to brown the top of the omelet.
4 Cut across the center of the omelet (don't cut right through it), spoon your chosen filling (see below) over one half, then fold over the other half. Lift the omelet out of the skillet and serve.
SERVES 1

SAVOURY FILLINGS

1 ASPARAGUS

Boil or steam 2–4 asparagus spears until just tender then cut them into 1-inch lengths.

2 BELL PEPPER

Broil ½ red or yellow bell pepper, or a combination, until charred then peel off the skin and slice thinly.

3 MUSHROOM

Wash, dry and slice ½ cup mushrooms – any type, or a mixture – then sauté them in 1 tablespoon of butter until they are tender and any liquid they produce has boiled away (this may take up to 15 minutes). Season with salt and pepper.

4 CHEESE

Mix 2 tablespoons of grated cheese with the egg yolks, then sprinkle another 2 tablespoons on top of the omelet just before you fold it. Gruyère or Parmesan, or a mixture, are good.

5 RATATOUILLE

Leftover ratatouille (see page 40) makes a very good filling; reheat gently, allowing 2 heaped tablespoons per omelet.

6 TRUFFLE

For a luxurious treat, put a few truffle shavings on top of the omelet before folding it.

7 PEAS AND MINT

Cook ⅓ cup fresh or frozen peas in a little boiling water for 2 minutes. Drain, add a little butter and 2 teaspoons of chopped fresh mint.

SWEET FILLINGS

1 FRESH FRUIT

Any sweet, soft-textured fruit is good, such as blackberries or blueberries, sliced sweet ripe mango, or sliced banana with a sprinkling of cinnamon. Or use ½ cup strawberries or other red berries, sliced and sprinkled with sugar and 1 tablespoon of liqueur: try Cointreau with strawberries or kirsch with cherries.

2 JAM

Melt 1 tablespoon of jam in a small pan over a gentle heat – apricot or black cherry are especially good. You could also add a dash of liqueur.

3 PRESERVED FRUIT

Use 2 tablespoons of fruits preserved in liqueur, or coarsely chopped preserved stem ginger.

SPANISH OMELET

This simple flat omelet is wonderfully tasty and filling, and like all flat omelets it can be eaten hot, warm or cold. Any that's left over is delicious the next day, reheated and served with a fresh tomato sauce or served hot or cold with salad.

2 pounds potatoes	**3 tbls olive oil**
1 large onion or	**salt and freshly ground**
1 bunch of	**black pepper**
scallions	**6 eggs**

1. Half fill a saucepan with water and put it on the stove to heat up. Peel the potatoes, cut them into chunks about ½ inch square then add them to the pan and boil for 6–8 minutes or until just tender. Drain and set aside.

2. Meanwhile, peel and finely chop the onion or trim and chop the scallions. Heat 2 tablespoons of the olive oil in a heavy-based 8-inch skillet and then put in the onion. Cover and cook until tender: 7–8 minutes for the onion, 2–3 minutes for the scallions.

3. Add the potatoes to the skillet, stirring to mix all the ingredients together and adding some salt and pepper to taste. Leave the vegetables to cook gently while you beat the eggs with a little salt and pepper.

4. Pour the eggs into the skillet. Cook the omelet gently until it is lightly browned underneath and looks set on top, about 5–10 minutes.

5. Invert a large plate over the skillet and turn the omelet out on to it. Heat the remaining oil in the pan then slide the omelet back in to cook the other side: this will take about 3–4 minutes. Serve cut into wedges.

SERVES 4

VARIATION

MIXED VEGETABLE OMELET

De-seed and chop 1 green bell pepper and fry it with the onion. Boil ⅔ cup frozen peas with the potatoes, adding them a couple of minutes before the end of the cooking time.

Spanish omelet makes a good appetizer, cut into small squares and accompanied by a spicy dipping sauce.

SWISS CHARD FRITTATA

6 eggs
1 cup grated cheese,
  (Parmesan, Gruyère
  or a mixture)
3–4 tbs chopped fresh
  basil or parsley

salt and freshly
  ground black pepper
3 tbs olive oil
8 ounces Swiss chard,
  without stalks

1 Beat the eggs and stir in three quarters of the cheese, plus the herbs and some salt and pepper.
2 Heat 2 tablespoons of the olive oil in a large saucepan, put in the chard and stir-fry for 1–2 minutes until wilted. Be careful not to let it burn.
3 Heat the remaining oil in an 8-inch skillet and tip in the chard, spreading it over the pan – it will still be very springy and leafy. Then pour the eggs on top of the leaves. Check that the mixture isn't sticking to the bottom of the skillet, then cover and cook over the lowest possible heat for about 15 minutes, until set.
4 Heat the broiler. Sprinkle the remaining cheese over the frittata and place under the broiler for 1–2 minutes to cook the top. Serve cut into wedges.
SERVES 4

SUMMER FRITTATA

8 ounces tender
  asparagus spears
8 ounces zucchini
8 sun-dried tomatoes
  in oil, drained
4 eggs
⅓ cup grated
  Parmesan cheese

2 tbs chopped fresh
  parsley
salt and freshly
  ground black pepper
2 tbs olive oil

OPPOSITE: *(left) Cheese and Herb Omelet, page 34, (top) Mushroom Soufflé Omelet, page 35, (right) Vegetable Frittata with Mint Sauce*

1 Trim the asparagus and cut the zucchini into ¼-inch slices. Cook the vegetables in a little boiling water for a few minutes until tender but slightly crunchy. Drain immediately.
2 Heat the broiler. Chop the sun-dried tomatoes. Whisk the eggs lightly, add the cheese, tomatoes and parsley and season with a little salt and pepper.
3 Heat the oil in an 8-inch skillet, add the vegetables then pour in the egg mixture. Cook for 4–5 minutes, until the bottom of the frittata is set and golden brown, then put the skillet under the broiler and leave for a further minute or two to set the top. Serve cut in half or in thick wedges.
SERVES 2

VEGETABLE FRITTATA WITH MINT SAUCE

8 ounces cauliflower
1 carrot
1 cup peas
4 eggs
salt and freshly
  ground black pepper

1 tbs butter

FOR THE MINT SAUCE
a large bunch of mint
1 tbs honey
1 tbs wine vinegar

1 First make the mint sauce: wash the mint and remove any tough stalks, then chop the leaves in a food processor or by hand and add the honey and vinegar. Put into a bowl to serve with the frittata.
2 Wash the cauliflower and cut it into flowerets then scrape and slice the carrot. Cook the vegetables in 2 inches of boiling water for about 4 minutes, until just tender, then drain and return to the still-warm pan. Stir in the peas.
3 Heat the broiler. Whisk the eggs lightly and season with salt and pepper.
4 Melt the butter in an 8-inch skillet, add the vegetables then pour in the eggs. Cook for 4–5 minutes, until set and golden brown underneath, then put under the broiler for 1–2 minutes to set the top. Serve cut into wedges, with the mint sauce.
SERVES 2

You won't need the thick, juicy stalks from the chard for this recipe: these are excellent cooked in boiling water until just tender then served with butter and/or shavings of Parmesan, or in a light cheese sauce. If you can't get Swiss chard you can make the frittata with spinach.

37

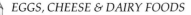
CREPES

✳

Any leftover crêpes freeze well: interleave them with wax paper and wrap in foil so that you can take them out singly. A stack of crêpes in the freezer makes any of these recipes practical for one person.

BASIC CREPE RECIPE

1 cup flour – white or half white and half whole wheat

2 eggs

2 tbs oil or melted butter, plus extra for frying

1¼ cups skim milk or milk and water

1 If you've got a blender or food processor, put in the flour, eggs, oil or melted butter and milk and whizz to a batter. If not, put the flour into a bowl and beat in the eggs, oil or butter and about a third of the milk. Mix until smooth, then gradually beat in the rest of the milk. The batter should be the consistency of light cream.

2 Put a 6-inch skillet over a low heat and brush it with a little oil or melted butter: a good way to do this is with a pad of paper towels.

3 When the skillet is hot enough to sizzle if a drop of water is flicked into it, pour in 2 tablespoons of batter and tilt the pan to cover the base.

4 Fry for 1–2 minutes until the top is set then, using a metal spatula and your fingers, flip the crêpe over and cook the other side for a few seconds. Cook the remaining crêpes in the same way, brushing the pan with oil or butter between every couple of crêpes. As the crêpes are done, stack them up on a plate, cover them with another plate and keep them warm over a pan of steaming water.

SERVES 4

Crêpes are delicious wrapped around a tasty filling then sprinkled with cheese and browned quickly under the broiler. If you have more time you could make a thin cheese sauce (see page 67) and pour this over the crêpes before broiling. Serve with a simple salad and a cooked vegetable for a satisfying meal.

VARIATIONS

1 HERB CREPES

Add 2 tablespoons of chopped fresh herbs to the batter.

2 ORANGE OR LEMON CREPES

Add the grated rind of 1 orange or lemon and 1 tablespoon of sugar to the batter.

3 CHOCOLATE CREPES

Mix 1 tablespoon of unsweetened cocoa powder and 1 tablespoon of sugar in with the batter.

SPINACH AND STILTON CREPES

crêpe batter (see above)

2 pounds fresh spinach

8 ounces Stilton cheese

salt and freshly ground black pepper

1 Make the crêpes as described above.

2 Wash the spinach, then cook it in a dry pan for about 7–10 minutes, until it is tender. Drain well.

3 Heat the broiler. Crumble or grate the cheese and add half to the spinach, then season with salt and pepper. Spread a little of this mixture on to each crêpe and roll it up. Put the crêpes side by side in a shallow heatproof dish then sprinkle with the rest of the cheese.

4 Put the crêpes under the broiler for a few minutes until the cheese on top has melted and everything is bubbling hot. Serve at once.

SERVES 4

VARIATION

CREPES WITH BOURSIN CHEESE

Mash 2 cups Boursin cheese with a little milk, then spread this on the crêpes and roll them up loosely. Sprinkle with ⅔ cup finely grated Parmesan cheese and brown under the broiler.

OPPOSITE: *Crêpes Suzette with Berries, page 41*

RED CABBAGE, APPLE AND RAISIN CREPES

*crêpe batter (see
    page 38)*
1 pound red cabbage
1 apple
2 tbs olive oil
*1 onion, peeled and
    chopped*
*salt and freshly
    ground black pepper*
⅓ cup raisins
*½ cup grated Cheddar
    cheese*
*sour cream
    (optional)*

The red cabbage mixture can cook for longer than 15 minutes, if you've got time, and will just go on improving as long as it doesn't stick. If there's any over, it's lovely with baked potatoes and sour cream: in fact, it's almost worth making extra for this.

1. Make the crêpes as described on page 38.
2. Wash the red cabbage and shred it as finely as you can. Chop the apple. Heat the oil in a pan and put in the cabbage, apple and onion. Add a sprinkling of salt and the raisins, cover and cook for 10–15 minutes, until tender. Stir occasionally and add 1–2 tablespoons of water if the mixture starts to stick.
3. Season the cabbage mixture well, then spoon it on to the crêpes and roll them up. Put the crêpes side by side in a shallow heatproof dish then sprinkle over the grated cheese.
4. Put the crêpes under a hot broiler for a few minutes until the cheese has melted and everything is bubbling hot. Serve at once, topped with a spoonful of sour cream, if you are using this.

SERVES 4

RATATOUILLE CREPES

*herb crêpe batter (see
    page 38)*
1 tbs olive oil
*1 onion, peeled and
    chopped*
1 red bell pepper
*1 eggplant, about 8–12
    ounces*
8 ounces zucchini
*1¾ cups canned
    tomatoes*
1 garlic clove, crushed
*salt and freshly
    ground black pepper*
*⅔ cup finely grated
    Parmesan cheese,*

1. Make the crêpes as described on page 38.
2. Heat the oil in a pan, add the onion and start to cook this over a moderate heat.
3. Meanwhile, halve, de-seed and chop the red bell pepper and add this to the onion. Chop the eggplant and the zucchini and add these to the pan. Finally add the garlic. Cover the pan and cook gently for 5 minutes.
4. Add the tomatoes and their juice, breaking them up with a spoon. Simmer for 15–20 minutes until all the vegetables are tender and the liquid has reduced. Season with salt and pepper then spoon this mixture on to the crêpes and roll them up. Put the crêpes side by side in a shallow heatproof dish then sprinkle over the Parmesan cheese.
5. Put the crêpes under a hot broiler for a few minutes until the cheese has melted and everything is bubbling hot. Serve at once.

SERVES 4

VARIATION

CHILI CREPES

These are nice served with some guacamole and sour cream, or a chopped avocado salad. Increase the amount of tomatoes to 2 cups and substitute 1¾ cups canned red kidney beans for the zucchini. Cook as above, seasoning the mixture with a good pinch of chili powder. Substitute Cheddar cheese for the Parmesan.

CHOCOLATE AND CHERRY CREPES

These are best made with fresh, ripe black cherries, which you need to pit. Wear rubber gloves so your nails don't get stained and use a cherry pitter or a sharp knife.

1 pound ripe black cherries	**chocolate crêpe batter (see page 38)**
sugar	**⅔ cup sour cream**
dash of kirsch	

1 Pit the cherries then put them into a bowl and sprinkle with a little sugar and a dash of kirsch.

2 Make the crêpes as described on page 38.

3 Spread the crêpes with the sour cream and top with the cherries. Roll them up, sprinkle with sugar and serve.

SERVES 4

CREPES SUZETTE WITH BERRIES

These are wonderful for a quick special dessert but I also like them as an unconventional light meal.

orange crêpe batter (see page 38)	**4 tbs orange-flavored liqueur such as Cointreau or Grand Marnier, or brandy**
½ cup sweet butter	
⅔ cup freshly squeezed orange juice	**¼ cup blueberries**
grated rind of 1 orange	
½ cup sugar	

1 Make the crêpes as described on page 38, using melted butter to grease the skillet.

2 Gently melt the sweet butter in a large skillet and then add the orange juice and rind, sugar and half the liqueur or brandy. Heat this mixture gently.

3 Place one crêpe in the skillet and cook for a few seconds to heat it through. Fold it in half then in half again to make a triangle and push it to the far side of the skillet. Repeat this process with the remaining crêpes. Sprinkle the blueberries into the pan.

4 Put the remaining liqueur or brandy into a metal ladle or a small saucepan and warm it over a flame or on the stove. When it is tepid, set it alight with a match, standing well back and averting your face. Pour it over the crêpes and serve immediately.

SERVES 4

APPLE CREPES

Although sweet crêpes are usually served as a dessert, I rather like to have them occasionally as a light main course, instead of at the end of a meal when I feel too full to enjoy them. A dessert and a pot of black coffee make a pleasant meal occasionally!

orange crêpe batter (see page 38)	**sugar**
1 pound sweet, mellow dessert apples	**⅓ cup raisins (optional)**
1 tbs butter	

1 Make the crêpes as described on page 38.

2 Peel and core the apples and slice them thinly. Melt the butter in a saucepan, add the apples, a little sugar, and the raisins if you are using them, and stir to mix together. Cook, uncovered, over a low heat, stirring gently from time to time, for about 3–4 minutes or until the apple slices have softened and become tender.

3 Spoon this mixture on to the crêpes and roll them up. Sprinkle with a little sugar and then serve them immediately, perhaps with some crème fraîche.

SERVES 4

These crêpes are particularly delicious if you add to the apple mixture a good pinch of cinnamon and/or ground cloves or a splash of Calvados or brandy.

CHEESE SALADS

ROQUEFORT SALAD

1 red-leaf lettuce
1 tbs rice vinegar
1 tbs olive oil
salt and freshly
  ground black pepper

1–2 tbs snipped fresh
  chives
4 ounces Roquefort
  cheese

1   Wash the lettuce and put the leaves in a salad spinner or colander to drain.
2   Put the rice vinegar, oil and some seasoning into a salad bowl and mix. Then put in the chives. Tear the lettuce roughly on top.
3   Cut or break the Roquefort into pieces and add to the bowl, then gently toss the salad to coat the leaves with dressing and distribute the ingredients.
SERVES 2

BROCCOLI, CHERRY TOMATO AND FETA SALAD

1 tbs olive oil
1 tbs rice vinegar
salt and freshly
  ground black pepper
8 ounces cherry
  tomatoes

4 scallions
4 ounces feta cheese
1 pound broccoli
a few sprigs of
  oregano

1   Put the oil, vinegar and some seasoning into a salad bowl. Halve the tomatoes, trim and chop the scallions and put them in the bowl. Break the feta into rough chunks and add to the bowl, too.

OPPOSITE: (left) Broccoli, Cherry Tomato and Feta Salad, (top) Warm Carrot and Goat Cheese Salad, (right) Roquefort Salad

2   Wash the broccoli and separate it into small flowerets. Peel and slice the stems. Cook, covered, in 1 inch of boiling water for 4 minutes, then drain immediately into a strainer, pat dry with paper towels and add to the other ingredients in the bowl.
3   Tear the oregano over the top, mix gently and serve the salad at once, while it is still warm.
SERVES 2

WARM CARROT AND GOAT CHEESE SALAD

The idea for this came from an excellent quiche I ate at Stephen Bull's restaurant in London. I loved the combination of ingredients, which I have recreated as this salad, adding a thyme and honey vinaigrette.

7 ounces firm goat
  cheese
8 sun-dried tomatoes
  in oil, drained
1 pound carrots
2 tbs oil from the sun-
  dried tomatoes
4 tsp clear honey

2 tbs balsamic
  vinegar
½ tsp dried thyme or
  1 tsp chopped fresh
  thyme
salt and freshly
  ground black pepper
sprigs of fresh thyme

1   Cut the goat cheese into ¼-inch dice and put it into a bowl. Chop the sun-dried tomatoes and add these to the bowl, too.
2   Scrape the carrots and slice them very thinly – the side of a grater or a mandoline is good for this. Cook in a little boiling water for 1 minute; drain, pat dry with paper towels and add to the bowl.
3   Add the oil, honey, vinegar, thyme, a little salt and a grinding or two of pepper and mix well. Garnish with the sprigs of thyme then serve at once, while the carrots are still warm.
SERVES 2–4

I like rice vinegar because it's light and sweet, so you can use less oil in the dressing and thus reduce the dreaded calories.

CHEESE DIP WITH CRUDITES

In my experience this is very popular with children and teenagers – and it's also a good way of encouraging them to eat more vegetables, since they can choose their favorite raw vegetables to eat with it.

about 12 ounces raw vegetables: sticks of cucumber, carrot and celery; small flowerets of cauliflower; cherry tomatoes, radishes, scallions; crisp lettuce, etc.	*2 tbs low-fat soft white cheese or plain yogurt, or 2 tbs milk and 1 tbs soft butter freshly ground black pepper*
2 ounces Cheddar or other hard cheese	

1. Prepare the vegetables, cutting them into pieces suitable for dipping.
2. Finely grate the cheese. Put it into a bowl with the soft cheese, yogurt, or milk and butter and beat them together until creamy.
3. Season with pepper, then spoon into a small dish and put this on a plate or into a shallow basket, surrounded by the vegetables. Or you can spoon the dip straight on to a plate and arrange the vegetables around it.

SERVES 1

A REALLY GOOD PLOUGHMAN'S

A traditional British ploughman's lunch can be delicious, although in my experience the ones you get in pubs often aren't: hunks of boring bread and cheese, syrupy brown pickles, some tired lettuce and tomato, and a spoonful of synthetic-tasting coleslaw. But choose the cheese with care and serve it with good, warm bread, fresh, crisp salad and interesting pickles, and it's a feast.

fresh, crusty bread, white, whole wheat or multigrain butter (optional) 2–4 ounces good-quality aged Cheddar or Stilton cheese	*crisp lettuce leaves 1 firm tomato, sliced pickled onions or other pickles*

1. Warm the bread, then cut it into thick slices and arrange on a platter with the remaining ingredients. Serve with a glass of beer or apple cider.

SERVES 1

VARIATIONS

1 FRENCH PLOUGHMAN'S

Use good French bread – either a baguette or French country bread – and a French cheese of your choice: Brie or a firm goat cheese would be fine. Add a handful of black olives, some salad leaves such as field lettuce or endive, and plum tomatoes. Serve with French red country wine.

2 GREEK PLOUGHMAN'S

The basis of this variation is some crumbly, salty feta cheese and some Kalamata olives. Serve with soft, country-style bread and a tomato and onion salad, and drink some chilled white wine with it.

3 GERMAN PLOUGHMAN'S

Choose a dark rye bread, such as pumpernickel, and cheese flavored with caraway or cumin seeds or paprika. Serve with pickled cucumbers.

GOAT CHEESE SALAD

In fashionable circles this is now regarded as a bit of a has-been, but really it's a classic and so quick, as well as being one of my personal favorites. It's best if the goat cheese is the same width as the baguette.

2 cups mixed salad leaves	4 ounces firm goat cheese
fresh herbs, if available; chervil is especially good	1 tsp balsamic vinegar
	1 tbs olive oil
2–4 thin slices of baguette	salt and freshly ground black pepper

1. Wash the salad leaves, shake them dry and put them into a bowl with some torn-up herbs, if you have them.
2. Lightly toast the baguette slices on one side under the broiler.
3. Cut the goat cheese into 2 or 4 slices and place on the untoasted side of the baguette, then put them under the broiler until the cheese is brown and bubbling.
4. Meanwhile, sprinkle the vinegar and oil over the salad with a little salt and pepper and toss the leaves. Cut the pieces of baguette in half, put them on top of the salad, and serve at once.

SERVES 1

NO-COOK CHEESE FEASTS

With the excellent cheeses, breads, fruit and vegetables that are now widely available, you can put together a wonderful feast that requires no cooking and hardly any preparation – just a bit of careful shopping. Here are some good combinations: you could serve one or several at a time, depending on the number of people. Some red or white wine (or fruit juice spritzers) would complete the spread. You need to allow about 4 ounces of cheese per person.

1 APPLES AND CHEDDAR

Choose really good apples with melting, sweet flesh – mature McIntoshes or Red Delicious, for instance – and a good-quality aged Cheddar. Some whole wheat bread, especially the home-made, rather heavy, moist type, goes well with this.

2 VIGNOTTE OR CAMEMBERT AND GRAPES

This is a gorgeous combination, more like a dessert than a main course. Choose the best grapes available – perhaps a mixture of two colors – and some crumbly oatcakes.

3 PEAR WITH GORGONZOLA OR PECORINO

Buttery, sweet ripe pears – preferably Comice – with either Gorgonzola or Pecorino cheese, and perhaps some peppery watercress or arugula leaves and good plain Italian bread.

4 RICOTTA, BLUE CHEESE AND CELERY

Two contrasting cheeses and crisp, clean-tasting celery stalks make a good combination. Serve either warm, crusty bread or some thin crackers to accompany them.

5 INSALATA TRICOLORE

Slice some good-quality, water-packed Mozzarella cheese – preferably buffalo Mozzarella – and arrange it on a plate with sliced plum or beefsteak tomatoes, slices of ripe avocado tossed in lemon juice, and torn leaves of fresh basil. Serve this classic salad with warm Italian bread.

6 CREAM CHEESE WITH RIPE PINEAPPLE

The success of this depends more than anything on the quality of the pineapple. If you can get a really ripe, sweet, juicy one, it can be superb. Peel the pineapple, removing all the little tufts and the inner core, then cut it into chunks or slices and arrange on a plate with the cheese. You could use mascarpone or a cream cheese from the deli: both regular and lighter varieties are fine.

For an even quicker cheese salad that never seems to go out of fashion, mash ¼ cup of blue cheese with 4 tablespoons of yogurt or sour cream, season to taste then spoon on top of Bibb lettuce, cut into chunks.

Pineapples are usually ready to eat when they smell slightly syrupy and one of the inner leaves pulls out easily.

FRIED, MELTED & BROILED CHEESE

---✳---

HALOUMI WITH SPICED LEEKS

Moist, tender leeks spiced up with cumin seed and the sharp tang of lime make a delicious base for crisp slices of haloumi cheese. Haloumi is firm, so you can fry it without it melting. However, if you can't find it, use a firm mozzarella or feta cheese. Serve this with a salad, bread or rice. Basmati rice will cook quickly while you're preparing the haloumi mixture.

Haloumi is an unusual cheese because it is very firm and keeps its shape well when broiled or fried. Read the packet to make sure you're getting a vegetarian one. Unopened, it keeps for ages in the fridge and for even longer in the freezer.

1½ pounds young, tender leeks	juice of 1 lime
8 ounces haloumi cheese	salt and freshly ground black pepper
2 tbs olive oil	
½ tsp cumin seeds	

1 Slice the leeks fairly finely. Cut the cheese into slices about ⅓ inch thick then cut each slice in half to make squarish pieces.

2 Heat the oil in a skillet, put in the cheese and fry for 1–2 minutes until golden brown on one side, then flip the pieces over and fry the other side. This whole process only takes 2–3 minutes.

3 Drain the cheese on paper towels.

4 Put the leeks into the skillet and stir-fry for about 5 minutes or until they are just tender. Then add the cumin seeds and stir for a moment or two longer. Add the lime juice and seasoning.

5 Put the cheese back into the skillet with the leeks and heat through for a few minutes. Serve on warm plates.

SERVES 2

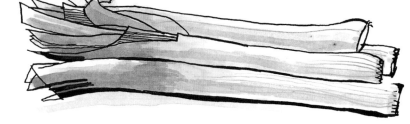

HALOUMI AND ZUCCHINI WITH TOMATO SALSA

8 ounces tomatoes	12 ounces zucchini
½ onion, peeled and chopped	8 ounces haloumi cheese
2 tbs chopped fresh cilantro	3 tbs olive oil
salt and freshly ground black pepper	

1 First make the salsa: pour boiling water over the tomatoes, leave for a few seconds, then drain and cover with cold water. Slip off the skins with a sharp knife then chop the tomatoes and put them into a bowl. Add the onion, cilantro and some salt and pepper to taste.

2 Wash and thinly slice the zucchini. Cut the cheese into slices about ⅓ inch thick then cut each slice in half to make squarish pieces.

3 Heat 2 tablespoons of the oil in a skillet, put in the zucchini and fry for 3–4 minutes or until they are tender and golden brown in patches. Then remove them from the skillet and keep them warm.

4 Heat the remaining oil in the skillet, put in the cheese and fry for 1–2 minutes, until it is golden brown on one side. Then flip the pieces over and fry the other side. This whole process only takes 2–3 minutes.

5 Put the zucchini back in the skillet, mix with the haloumi and turn gently to make sure everything is really hot. Serve on to plates and top with the salsa.

SERVES 2

OPPOSITE: *Haloumi with Spiced Leeks*

DEEP-FRIED CAMEMBERT

If you're just making this for one or two people the cheese can be fried in a medium saucepan in a relatively small amount of oil, saving the hassle of using a deep-fat fryer. Serve with green salad leaves, if you like; the combination of hot, melted cheese and cool, crisp leaves is particularly good. I like some sweet mango chutney or apricot jam with it, too.

1 small wheel of Camembert cheese cut into 4 wedges, and chilled in the fridge

1 egg, beaten with 1 tbs water
dry breadcrumbs for coating
oil for deep-frying

1 Dip the pieces of Camembert into the beaten egg, then into the crumbs to coat them. Repeat the process so that they are really well coated then chill them in the fridge again while you heat the oil.

2 Half-fill a saucepan with oil and heat it. Test the temperature by dipping a wooden chopstick or the handle of a wooden spoon into it: the oil should immediately form bubbles around it.

3 Put in the pieces of Camembert and fry for 4–5 minutes, until they are crisp and golden brown. Remove them with a draining spoon and put them on crumpled paper towels to absorb excess oil. Serve immediately.

SERVES 2

CHEESE FONDUE

Cheese fondue is very quick to make. It can be served from the pan without using a fondue burner, or simply poured over warm French bread, though I think it's more fun to eat if you dip the bread into it. You can make fondue for one person but it's more enjoyable when you're sharing it.

1 baguette
1 garlic clove, halved
8 ounces Swiss cheese, such as Emmenthal
⅔ cup dry white wine or apple cider

2 tsp cornstarch
1 tsp lemon juice
salt and freshly ground black pepper
freshly grated nutmeg

1 Cut or break the bread into bite-sized pieces, spread them out on a cookie sheet or heatproof dish and put them under a not-too-hot broiler to warm.

2 Rub the garlic around the inside of a medium-sized saucepan, then discard it. Grate the cheese.

3 Put all but 1 tablespoon of the wine or apple cider into the saucepan, add the cheese and bring just to the boil – the cheese will look like a lumpy mess at this stage but don't worry.

4 Blend the cornstarch with the remaining wine or apple cider, then pour this into the cheese mixture, stirring vigorously over the heat. The mixture will thicken and become smooth.

5 Remove from the heat and add the lemon juice and some salt, pepper and grated nutmeg to taste. Serve at once with the warm bread, and have long forks available so that you can spear pieces of bread and dip them into the fondue in the pan.

SERVES 2

You can vary the fondue by using different cheeses: try Cheddar and beer for a very British flavor, or blue cheese with apple cider or a fruity white wine.

MELTED BRIE WITH ALMONDS

This is very easy and makes a good quick meal served with a crisp leafy salad or a tomato salad.

8–12 ounces Brie
¼ cup slivered almonds

1 Slice the Brie, including the rind, and arrange it in a shallow layer in a heatproof dish.
2 Place the dish under a hot broiler for about 5–7 minutes, until the Brie has begun to melt, then sprinkle the almonds evenly on top and broil for a few more minutes, until the nuts have toasted. Watch it carefully because they will burn quickly. Serve at once.
SERVES 2

BROILED FETA WITH OLIVES

This quick supper dish needs to be served with plenty of soft, plain bread – no butter – and some salad leaves.

8 ounces feta cheese   **⅓ cup large green**
⅓ cup black olives,   **olives**
** preferably Kalamata**

1 Heat the broiler. Cut the feta cheese into cubes and put them into a shallow heatproof dish. Add the olives, distributing them amongst the cheese.
2 Heat under the broiler for about 5 minutes, or until the feta is melting and has become golden brown in places. Serve at once.
SERVES 2

CHEESY TOMATO GRATIN

A good recipe for when you're on a diet or watching your fat intake. You can leave the Parmesan out if you want to reduce the fat and calories even further, but it is only a very small amount and it does add a lot of flavor. Peppery salad ingredients such as watercress or arugula go well with this, or some quickly steamed broccoli or French beans.

1 beefsteak tomato   **1½ tbs grated**
salt and freshly   **Parmesan cheese**
** ground black pepper**
a few fresh basil
** leaves**
½ cup non-fat cottage
** cheese, plain or with**
** chives and/or onion**

1 Heat the broiler. Slice the tomato into thick rounds. Place these in a shallow ovenproof dish in a single layer, season with salt and pepper and tear over some basil leaves.
2 Spoon the cottage cheese evenly over the tomato, then sprinkle with the Parmesan cheese.
3 Broil for about 10 minutes, or until everything is heated through and the top is golden brown.
SERVES 1

DESSERTS WITH CHEESE, CREAM & YOGURT

_____ ✳ _____

CHOCOLATE AMARETTI PIE

This is a very quick chocolate pie, consisting of a crumb crust with a light, creamy chocolate topping. You can eat it almost immediately or leave it overnight – it just gets better all the time! It's a useful emergency dessert because the ingredients are so simple, but it is essential that you use good-quality bittersweet chocolate.

**10 ounces bittersweet
    chocolate, at least
    50% cocoa solids
2 tbs butter
4 ounces amaretti
    cookies**

**⅞ cup light cream
½ tsp finely grated
    orange rind
slivers of orange rind
    to decorate**

1 First make a start on the topping: break two-thirds of the chocolate into pieces and put them into a deep bowl set over a pan of steaming water. Leave until the chocolate has melted then remove the bowl from the pan and stand it in a bowl of cold water to cool it down quickly.

2 While the chocolate is melting, make the base, but first draw a vegetable parer down the length of the remaining chocolate to make a few chocolate curls for decorating the pie; keep these on one side. Break the rest of the chocolate into pieces, put them into a medium saucepan with the butter and melt over a very low heat.

3 Crush the amaretti cookies, then remove the chocolate mixture from the heat and stir in the cookie crumbs until they are well coated.

4 Spoon the crumb mixture into a 7–8-inch plain tart pan with a removable rim, pressing the mixture down firmly with the back of a spoon. Put it in a cool place (I put mine in the freezer).

5 Now pour the cream into the bowl of melted chocolate, add the grated orange rind and whisk until thick and pale. This will only take a few minutes if the mixture is cold enough: if it takes longer, put it in the fridge or freezer for a few minutes.

6 Spoon the chocolate cream into the tart pan, taking it right to the edges and smoothing the top with the back of the spoon. You can serve it almost immediately or refrigerate it. Run a knife around the edges and remove the tart rim, neatening the

edges with the knife – the longer you leave it the easier it will be to turn out. Decorate the top with the reserved chocolate curls and the orange strands before serving. It's nice as it is, or with some extra light cream, or with cream lightly whipped with 1 tablespoon of rum, brandy or Amaretto liqueur.
SERVES 4–6

THICK YOGURT WITH FRESH DATES

This is my slightly adapted version of one of Prue Leith's ideas. As she says, the better the quality of the ingredients you use, the better the dessert will be.

**⅓ cup almonds
1½ cups fresh dates
2 cups thick strained
    yogurt**

**4 tbs heavy cream
4 tbs clear honey**

1 First blanch the almonds: put them into a small saucepan, cover with water and boil for 1 minute. Then remove from the heat, drain, and pop the nuts out of their skins. Chop them roughly.

2 Pit the dates and chop them roughly.

3 Put a few dates in the bottom of four glass bowls. Put 2 good heaped tablespoons of yogurt into each bowl then put the rest of the dates on top. Spoon the cream on top, then drizzle the honey over that and finally sprinkle over the chopped almonds.
SERVES 4

_____

OPPOSITE: *(left) Chocolate Amaretti Pie, (center) Ricotta Cream with Candied Fruit, page 52, (right) Thick Yogurt with Fresh Dates*

RICOTTA CREAM WITH CANDIED FRUIT

This is a nice dessert to make when there is some colorful candied fruit available. Vanilla sugar is easy to make, but if you haven't got any, use ordinary sugar and a few drops of real vanilla extract.

6 ounces mixed candied fruit	¾ cup ricotta cheese
2 tbs Marsala wine	1 tbs light cream
⅓ cup almonds	1 tbs vanilla sugar

1 Cut the candied fruit into fairly small pieces. Put them into a bowl and add the Marsala.

2 Put the almonds into a small saucepan, cover with water and boil for 1 minute. Then remove from the heat, drain, and pop the nuts out of their skins. Stir them into the fruit mixture.

3 Put the ricotta into a bowl and mix in the cream and vanilla sugar. Leave in a cool place until you want to serve the dessert. Stir the fruit again.

4 To serve, divide the ricotta mixture between two plates then spoon the fruit on to the plates.
SERVES 2

Vanilla sugar is wonderfully fragrant and flavorful, and is made by burying vanilla beans in granulated or confectioners' sugar – usually in the proportion of two beans for each pound of sugar. Store the mixture in an airtight container for about a week before removing the beans.

MASCARPONE LEMON CREAM

The lemon cuts the richness of the mascarpone in this delectable and easy dessert.

1 cup mascarpone cheese	2–4 tbs sugar
rind and juice of ½ lemon	slivers of lemon rind to decorate

1 Put the mascarpone cheese into a bowl with the lemon rind and juice and mix until smooth.

2 Mix in sugar to taste then spoon into dishes and decorate with slivers of lemon rind.
SERVES 2–3

A zester, which is inexpensive to buy, is invaluable for producing long strands of citrus rind quickly and easily.

COFFEE RICOTTA CREAM

Ricotta is a medium-fat cheese, so this isn't very high in calories; you could make it even less so by using a low-fat soft cheese, if you wish. A really good-quality instant espresso coffee will give this the best flavor.

1 cup ricotta cheese	chocolate-covered coffee beans, flakes of chocolate or toasted slivered almonds to decorate
1 tsp instant espresso coffee	
2–4 tbs sugar	

1 Put the ricotta cheese into a bowl and break it up with a spoon.

2 Dissolve the coffee in 1 tablespoon of hot water and add it to the ricotta, then add sugar to taste.

3 Mix until everything is well blended, then spoon into individual dishes and decorate with chocolate-covered coffee beans, a few flakes of chocolate or some toasted slivered almonds.
SERVES 2

YOGURT BRULEE

This can be as rich or as low in fat as you wish, depending on the type of yogurt you use and whether you add any cream. In any case, the crisp topping, which you have to smash with your spoon before eating the yogurt, makes it special.

1¼ cups plain low-fat yogurt, or creamy yogurt, or half plain yogurt and half heavy cream	⅓ cup sugar, plus extra to sweeten if desired

1 If you are using cream, whisk this until thick then fold in the yogurt. Sweeten to taste with a little sugar if you wish, remembering that the topping will add sweetness.

2 Spoon the yogurt or yogurt and cream into two ramekins, leaving some space at the top.

3 Put the sugar into a small saucepan and heat gently until it has turned to syrup and become golden brown – don't let it get too dark. Then immediately pour it over the yogurt. It will set hard within a few minutes; chill until needed.

SERVES 2

LIME CHEESECAKE

This is astonishingly quick to make, though it won't come to any harm if you keep it, well covered, in the fridge for several hours or even overnight. Some light cream and/or fresh fruit go well with it.

4 tbs butter	**4 tbs sugar**
6 ounces graham crackers	**2/3 cup heavy cream**
1 cup low-fat cream cheese	**thin slices of lime or slivers of rind and a few crushed pistachio nuts to decorate**
grated rind and juice of 1/2 lime	

1 First make the cheesecake base: melt the butter in a saucepan over a gentle heat; crush the graham crackers into crumbs. Stir the crumbs into the butter, off the heat, until they are well coated.

2 Spoon the crumbs into an 8-inch plain tart pan with a removable ring, pressing down with the back of the spoon. Put it in a cold place while you make the topping (I put mine in the freezer).

3 Put the cream cheese into a bowl with the lime rind and juice, sugar and heavy cream. Stir vigorously for 1–2 minutes, until very thick.

4 Spoon the filling on top of the base, taking it right to the edges. Decorate with lime slices or rind and pistachio nuts. You can serve it almost immediately, as it sets quickly, or leave it in the fridge. Run a knife around the edges and remove the tart ring, neatening the edges with the knife.

SERVES 4

QUICK CHOCOLATE WHIP

This can be whipped together in a few minutes and is a real treat, served in small glasses with some light, crisp cookies

10 ounces bittersweet chocolate, at least 50% cocoa solids	**flakes of bittersweet chocolate**
1¼ cups light cream	

1 Break the chocolate into pieces and put it into a deep bowl set over a pan of steaming water. Leave until the chocolate has melted then remove the bowl from the pan and put it in a cool place or in a bowl of cold water to cool it down quickly.

2 When the chocolate has cooled a little, pour in the light cream, which will cool it down further. Then whisk until the mixture gets thick and pale. This will only take a few minutes if the mixture is cold enough; if it takes longer, put it in the fridge or freezer for a few minutes.

3 Spoon the thick chocolate whip into glasses, decorate with the chocolate flakes and keep in the fridge or a cool place until required.

SERVES 4

VARIATION

1 RUM AND RAISIN CHOCOLATE WHIP

Before you start making the whip, put 1/3 cup raisins into a small bowl, cover with 2 tablespoons of rum and leave to plump up. Divide the raisins and any liquid that hasn't been absorbed between 4 glasses, then spoon the chocolate mixture on top.

To clean a pan in which sugar syrup has been made, leave the pan to cool then fill it with water and bring to the boil: this will dissolve the hard, sticky coating, making the pan easy to clean.

To crush cookies or crackers, put them into a large plastic bag and roll with a rolling pin.

PASTA

As long as you have a packet of pasta in the cupboard you can always rustle up a quick meal: pasta is good even when served simply with just olive oil or butter. If you add a few more ingredients and make sure you have plenty of different pasta shapes in your storecupboard, the scope is enormous. Dishes such as Quick Mediterranean Pasta, Fusilli with Fennel and Snow Peas, Spinach Tagliatelle with Walnuts and Fettuccine with Asparagus Sauce can all be made within 30 minutes, and they need little accompaniment – perhaps a simple salad or some bread – to make a satisfying meal.

TOMATO SAUCES
—— ✳ ——

QUICK MEDITERRANEAN PASTA

I like this with some full-bodied red wine and a leafy green salad containing arugula. Dress the salad with 2 teaspoons of red wine vinegar, 2 tablespoons of olive oil and some seasoning, and serve with the pasta.

1 tbs oil from the sun-dried tomatoes
1 onion, peeled and chopped
2 garlic cloves, crushed
1¾ cups canned tomatoes
8 sun-dried tomatoes in oil, drained
¾ cup canned artichoke hearts
⅓ cup black olives
salt and freshly ground black pepper
8 ounces penne rigate or rigatoni
6 fresh basil leaves
fresh Parmesan cheese, cut into slivers (optional)

1 First fill a saucepan with 2 quarts of water and bring to the boil for the pasta.
2 Meanwhile, heat the oil in a saucepan then add the onion, cover and cook gently for 10 minutes, until tender but not brown. Stir in the garlic and cook for 1–2 minutes longer.
3 Add the tomatoes, together with their juice, breaking them up with a wooden spoon. Chop the sun-dried tomatoes and add these to the pan too. Simmer for about 10–15 minutes, until the liquid has evaporated. Meanwhile, drain and slice the artichoke hearts and add these to the sauce along with the olives and plenty of salt and pepper.
4 When the water boils, add the pasta and let it bubble away, uncovered, for about 8 minutes or until it is *al dente*. Drain the pasta, return it to the pan and season with some salt; then add the sauce and stir so that all the pasta gets coated.
5 Tear the basil over the pasta, then serve topped with slivers of Parmesan cheese, if you like.
SERVES 2

SPAGHETTI WITH ROASTED BELL PEPPER AND TOMATO SAUCE

Roasted red bell pepper and sun-dried tomatoes give this a mellow, slightly sweet flavor; a leafy salad and some shavings of fresh Parmesan go perfectly with it.

1 red bell pepper
8 ounces spaghetti
1 onion, peeled and chopped
1 tbs oil from the sun-dried tomatoes
1–2 garlic cloves, crushed
1¾ cups canned tomatoes
4 sun-dried tomatoes in oil, drained
salt and freshly ground black pepper
fresh Parmesan cheese, cut into slivers

1 Cut the pepper into quarters, put it on a broiler pan cut-side down and broil under a high heat for about 10 minutes, until charred and blistered in places. Remove from the heat, cool slightly then peel off the skin and discard the stalk and seeds.
2 Fill a saucepan with 2 quarts of water and bring to the boil, then add the spaghetti and cook, uncovered, for about 8 minutes, until *al dente*.
3 Meanwhile, cook the onion gently in the oil for 10 minutes, until tender but not brown. Add the garlic and cook for 1–2 minutes longer, then stir in the canned tomatoes and their juice, breaking them up with a wooden spoon. Chop the sun-dried tomatoes and add these to the pan too. Simmer for about 10–15 minutes, until the liquid has evaporated.
4 Either put the sauce into a food processor with the red bell pepper and whizz to a purée, or chop the pepper and stir it into the sauce. Season well. Drain the pasta, return it to the saucepan and add some salt, then stir in the sauce so that all the pasta gets coated. Serve topped with slivers of Parmesan.
SERVES 2

OPPOSITE: *Quick Mediterranean Pasta*

PENNE WITH CHILI, TOMATO AND MUSHROOM SAUCE

The chili gives this sauce a kick while a splash of cream cools it down a bit, making a nice balance – though you could leave out either of them and the sauce would still be good.

2 cups small white mushrooms	8 ounces penne
1 green chili	4 tbs cream
1 tbs oil	salt and freshly
1 onion, peeled and chopped	ground black pepper
1 garlic clove, crushed	fresh Parmesan cheese, grated
1¼ cups canned tomatoes	

☐1 First fill a saucepan with 2 quarts of water and bring to the boil for the pasta.

☐2 Meanwhile, slice the mushrooms and halve, de-seed and chop the chili. Fry them in the oil in a large saucepan, along with the onion and garlic, for about 10 minutes, until softened but not brown.

☐3 Stir in the tomatoes and their juice, breaking them up with a wooden spoon, then simmer for 10–15 minutes, until the liquid has evaporated.

☐4 When the water boils, add the pasta and let it bubble away, uncovered, for about 8 minutes or until it is *al dente*. Meanwhile, stir the cream into the sauce and season it with salt and pepper.

☐5 Drain the pasta, return it to the still-warm saucepan and season with some salt. Then add the sauce and stir so that all the pasta gets coated. Serve out on to warm plates and hand round fresh Parmesan cheese separately.

SERVES 2

VARIATION

PENNE WITH PIQUANT SAUCE

This is a lively dish, particularly good on a cold night. Cook the pasta and make the tomato sauce as above, but omit the mushrooms, chili and cream. Instead, when the sauce is cooked, add ⅓ cup black olives, pitted and chopped, 1 tablespoon of capers, and a good pinch each of chili powder and cayenne pepper. Season with salt and pepper and add more chili or cayenne, if necessary. Serve with grated Parmesan.

FETTUCCINE WITH FRESH TOMATO SAUCE

This is at its best in the summer when made from flavorful fresh tomatoes.

1 tbs olive oil	salt and freshly
1 onion, peeled and chopped	ground black pepper
1 pound fresh tomatoes	6–8 fresh basil leaves
1 garlic clove, crushed	fresh Parmesan cheese, grated (optional)
8 ounces fettuccine or other delicate pasta	

☐1 First fill a saucepan with 2 quarts of water and bring to the boil for the pasta.

☐2 Next start making the sauce: heat the oil in a large saucepan then add the onion, cover and cook gently for 10 minutes, until tender but not brown.

☐3 Meanwhile, put the tomatoes in a bowl, cover with boiling water and leave for a few seconds until the skins loosen. Drain, cover with cold water and slip off the skins. Chop the tomatoes roughly, removing any hard bits of core.

☐4 Stir the garlic into the onion and cook for 1–2 minutes longer, then stir in the tomatoes and leave to cook, uncovered, for about 10–15 minutes, until the sauce is thick with no trace of wateriness.

☐5 When the water boils, add the fettuccine and let it bubble away, uncovered, for about 8 minutes or until it is *al dente*. Drain the pasta, return it to the pan and add the sauce. Season very well then mix together and tear the basil leaves over. Serve at once, with fresh Parmesan cheese if you like.

SERVES 2

For fresh tomato sauce, try to buy really ripe, tasty tomatoes, preferably vine-ripened ones. Shiny red plum tomatoes are usually good.

LIGHT PASTA DISHES

— ✳ —

PENNE WITH ROASTED PEPPERS AND ARUGULA

Roasted bell peppers, so moist and tender and sweet, make an excellent contrast to firm pasta, and the peppery arugula adds the final touch. If you can't get arugula, use some fresh basil leaves instead but add them straight to the cooked pasta; don't wilt them in the hot oil first.

1 large red bell pepper	2 tbs olive oil
1 large yellow bell pepper	salt and freshly ground black pepper
small handful of arugula	1 garlic clove, crushed
6 ounces penne, or similar-shaped pasta	fresh Parmesan cheese, cut into slivers (optional)

1 First prepare the peppers: cut them into quarters, put them on a broiler pan cut-side down and broil under a high heat until the skin has charred and blistered in places – this will take about 10 minutes and the pieces may need turning to make sure they cook evenly. When they are done, remove them from the heat and cover with a damp dish towel to cool them down and help loosen the skin.

2 Next fill a saucepan with 2 quarts of water and bring to the boil for the pasta.

3 Wash the arugula but don't chop it. Strip the skin off the peppers with a sharp knife, discard the stalks and seeds and cut the flesh into long, thin pieces.

4 When the water boils, add the pasta to the pan then let it bubble away, uncovered, for about 8 minutes or until it is *al dente*. Drain the pasta, return it to the still-warm saucepan and gently mix in 1 tablespoon of the oil and some salt to taste. Cover and keep warm.

5 Heat the remaining oil in another pan and put in the garlic, arugula and bell peppers; stir-fry for 1–2 minutes until everything is heated through, then tip the whole lot in with the pasta and toss well to combine. Check the seasoning and add some coarsely ground black pepper, then serve out on to warm plates and top with some slivers of Parmesan cheese if you wish.

SERVES 2

PASTA WITH PESTO

Pasta with pesto is delicious, and very quick to prepare using store-bought pesto. However, if you have a food processor you can easily whizz up your own. I like to use a long pasta such as spaghetti or tagliatelle and to serve it with a simple tomato and lettuce salad with a vinaigrette dressing.

8 ounces pasta	salt and freshly ground black pepper
1 cup fresh basil	
⅓ cup grated Parmesan cheese	fresh Parmesan cheese, grated, to serve
¼ cup pine nuts	
4 tbs olive oil	

1 Fill a saucepan with 2 quarts of water and put it on the stove to heat up for the pasta. When the water boils, add the pasta to the pan then let it bubble away, uncovered, for about 8 minutes or until it is *al dente*.

2 While the pasta is cooking, make the pesto: wash the basil and remove any large stalks then put the leaves into a food processor or blender along with the grated Parmesan cheese, pine nuts and olive oil. Whizz together briefly to make a bright green sauce.

3 Drain the pasta then put it back into the still-warm pan. Add the pesto, season well, then serve out on to warmed plates and hand round extra Parmesan cheese.

SERVES 2

PAPPARDELLE WITH PORCINI

Pappardelle is a particularly satisfying pasta – thick ribbons that you can really get your teeth into – and in this recipe it picks up the delicious flavor of the porcini mushrooms. Some extra shavings of fresh Parmesan make a nice finishing touch.

Dried porcini mushrooms - or ceps if you get the French ones - can be bought in tiny packets and are now stocked by large supermarkets. They can be used on their own or added to mushroom mixtures to intensify the flavor.

¼ cup dried porcini mushrooms	salt and freshly ground black pepper
8 ounces pappardelle or other ribbon pasta	fresh Parmesan cheese, cut into slivers
2 tbs butter	

1 Put the porcini into a small bowl and cover with boiling water. Leave on one side to soak.

2 Next fill a saucepan with 2 quarts of water and bring it to the boil. Add the pasta to the pan, then let it bubble away, uncovered, for about 8 minutes or until it is *al dente*.

3 Just before the pasta is ready, drain the porcini through a strainer lined with paper towels or cheesecloth and placed over a bowl. Chop the porcini finely, then put them into a small saucepan with their soaking liquid and boil for a few minutes until almost all the liquid has gone.

4 Drain the pasta then put it back into the still-warm pan with the butter, the porcini and some salt and pepper to taste. Mix gently, then serve out on to warmed plates and top with slivers of fresh Parmesan cheese.

SERVES 2

PASTA WITH FRESH HERBS

There are some excitingly flavored pastas around and these are fun to try for a change, although I must say they often look much more exotic than they taste. They are most effective when served simply. A flavored pasta – or a combination of two or three – is ideal in this recipe, although it is also delicious with plain pasta. Choose the herbs to complement the flavor of the pasta: basil for tomato; parsley and/or chives for mushroom; basil, parsley or chives for spinach; dill for beet; mixed herbs or perhaps something assertive like tarragon for plain pasta.

8 ounces pasta – perhaps a flavored one, or two or three different colors	2 tbs butter salt and freshly ground black pepper
bunch of fresh herbs	fresh Parmesan cheese, grated (optional)

1 First fill a saucepan with 2 quarts of water and bring to the boil. Add the pasta to the pan then let it bubble away, uncovered, for about 8 minutes or until it is *al dente*.

2 While the pasta is cooking, wash and chop the herbs – you need about 4 tablespoons.

3 Drain the pasta then put it back into the still-warm pan with the butter, herbs and some salt and pepper to taste. Mix gently, then serve out on to warmed plates, with fresh Parmesan if you wish.

SERVES 2

SUMMER SPAGHETTI WITH AVOCADO

This is good served with some hot garlic bread and a leafy summer salad.

1 pound tomatoes	1 avocado
6 ounces spaghetti	lemon juice
2 tbs olive oil	6–8 large basil leaves
1 garlic clove, crushed	freshly grated
salt and freshly ground black pepper	Parmesan cheese (optional)

1 First fill a saucepan with 2 quarts of water and bring to the boil for the pasta.

2 Put the tomatoes into a bowl, cover with boiling water and leave for a few seconds until the skins split. Drain, cover with cold water and slip off the skins with a sharp knife. Chop the tomatoes roughly, removing any hard bits of core.

3 When the water boils, add the spaghetti and cook, uncovered, for about 8 minutes, until *al dente*.

4 Heat the oil in a large saucepan, add the garlic and cook over a moderate heat for 1–2 minutes. Add the chopped tomatoes and salt and pepper to taste and heat gently, just to warm through. Peel, pit and chop the avocado and toss it in a little lemon juice.

5 Drain the pasta and return it to the still-warm saucepan. Add the tomato mixture and the avocado and toss well to mix, then tear in the basil, check the seasoning, and serve. Hand round Parmesan cheese separately, if you like.

SERVES 2

PASTA WITH GARLIC AND HERB MAYONNAISE

You can make this less rich by replacing some of the mayonnaise with plain yogurt, if you like. Summery and easy to prepare, it can be served either hot or cold. A simple salad goes well with it, and/or some warm bread.

8 ounces pasta, such as
   conchiglie
bunch of fresh herbs
4 tbs mayonnaise, a
   good bought one such
   as Hellmann's, or
   mayonnaise and
   plain yogurt mixed

1 garlic clove, crushed
salt and freshly
   ground black pepper
fresh Parmesan cheese,
   grated (optional)

1 First fill a saucepan with 2 quarts of water and bring to the boil. Add the pasta to the pan, then cook, uncovered, for about 8 minutes or until it is *al dente*.

2 While the pasta is cooking, wash and chop the herbs – you need about 4 tablespoons.

3 Drain the pasta then put it back into the still-warm pan. Add the mayonnaise, or mayonnaise and yogurt, and the herbs and garlic. Mix gently, season with salt and pepper, then serve out on to warmed plates, with fresh Parmesan if you wish.

SERVES 2

FUSILLI WITH FENNEL AND SNOW PEAS

8 ounces fennel bulb
4 ounces snow peas or
   sugar-snap peas
1 tbs butter
6 ounces fusilli or rotini

salt and freshly
   ground black pepper
fresh Parmesan cheese,
   grated (optional)

1 First fill a saucepan with 2 quarts of water and bring to the boil for the pasta.

2 Next prepare the vegetables: trim off any tough outer leaves and stalks from the fennel, reserving any green leafy bits for garnish. Wash and slice the fennel; wash and trim the snow peas.

3 Cook the fennel in 2 inches of boiling water for about 7 minutes, until it is almost tender, then put in the snow peas or sugar-snap peas and cook for a further 2 minutes. Drain, add the butter and leave on one side.

4 When the water boils, add the pasta to the pan, then let it bubble away, uncovered, for about 8 minutes or until it is *al dente*.

5 Just before the pasta is ready, gently reheat the vegetables, then drain the pasta and return it to the still-warm saucepan. Add the vegetables and snip in any reserved leafy bits of fennel. Check the seasoning and serve, with Parmesan cheese if you like.

SERVES 2

CAVATAPPI WITH SPINACH, RAISINS AND PINE NUTS

I love this mixture of contrasting flavors and textures; the sweetness of the raisins and the crunchiness of the toasted pine nuts complement the spinach and pasta perfectly. Cavatappi is a corkscrew-shaped pasta, but if you can't find it you can use fusilli or rotini instead.

1 pound tender fresh spinach or frozen leaf spinach	**¼ cup pine nuts**
2 tbs raisins	**salt and freshly ground black pepper**
3 tbs butter	**freshly grated nutmeg**
6 ounces cavatappi or similar pasta	**fresh Parmesan cheese, grated**

1   First fill a saucepan with 2 quarts of water and bring to the boil for the pasta.

2   Next prepare the spinach: if you are using fresh spinach, wash it in two or three changes of water and remove any tough stalks. Put the fresh or frozen spinach into a saucepan and cook over a high heat until the spinach has wilted and is tender. If the frozen spinach is very solid you may need to add a few tablespoons of water to the pan to prevent it sticking. Drain the spinach, add the raisins and half the butter and leave on one side until the pasta is done.

3   When the water boils, add the pasta to the pan, then let it bubble away, uncovered, for about 8 minutes or until it is *al dente*. While the pasta is cooking, toast the pine nuts under a hot broiler; keep your eye on them as they only take 1–2 minutes and can quickly burn. When they are golden brown, remove them from the broiler and keep on one side.

4   Just before the pasta is ready, gently reheat the spinach. Drain the pasta, return it to the still-warm saucepan with the rest of the butter and add the spinach mixture and the toasted pine nuts. Season with salt, pepper and freshly grated nutmeg and serve at once on to warmed plates. Hand round the Parmesan cheese separately.

SERVES 2

FUSILLI WITH ZUCCHINI AND TOMATOES

8 ounces zucchini	**1 garlic clove, crushed**
8 ounces tomatoes	**salt and freshly ground black pepper**
6 ounces fusilli or rotini	**6 large basil leaves**
2 tbs olive oil	**fresh Parmesan cheese**

1   First fill a saucepan with 2 quarts of water and bring to the boil for the pasta.

2   Next prepare the vegetables: wash the zucchini and cut them into rounds or matchsticks. Put the tomatoes into a bowl, cover with boiling water and leave for a few seconds until the skins split. Drain, cover with cold water and slip off the skins with a sharp knife. Chop the tomatoes into chunky pieces, removing any tough pieces around the stalk.

3   When the water boils, add the pasta to the pan, then let it bubble away, uncovered, for about 8 minutes or until it is *al dente*.

4   While the pasta is cooking, heat the oil in a large saucepan and add the zucchini and garlic. Cook over a moderate heat, stirring often, for about 4 minutes or until the zucchini are just tender, then add the tomatoes and salt and pepper to taste.

5   Just before the pasta is ready, gently reheat the zucchini mixture, then drain the pasta and return it to the still-warm saucepan. Stir the zucchini and tomatoes into the pasta; tear in the basil, check the seasoning, and top with some flaked or freshly grated Parmesan cheese.

SERVES 2

OPPOSITE: (top) *Spinach Tagliatelle with Walnuts, page 64, and (bottom) Fusilli with Zucchini and Tomatoes*

CHEESE & CREAM SAUCES

✳

SPINACH TAGLIATELLE WITH WALNUTS

This is a rich pasta dish which only needs a simple salad accompaniment: a fresh tomato and basil salad or a green salad, such as red-leaf lettuce, with a very light dressing would be nice.

1 tbs butter
1 onion, peeled and
  chopped
1 garlic clove, crushed
⅔ cup heavy
  cream

salt and freshly
  ground black pepper
8 ounces spinach
  tagliatelle
¼ – ½ cup chopped
  walnuts

To make a light balsamic vinegar vinaigrette to serve two people, mix 1 tablespoon of olive oil, 1 teaspoon of balsamic vinegar and some seasoning in a salad bowl. Put the salad leaves on top and toss just before you are ready to eat.

1. First fill a saucepan with 2 quarts of water and bring to the boil for the pasta.

2. Next start making the sauce: melt the butter in a small saucepan then put in the onion, cover and cook gently for 10 minutes, until tender but not brown. Stir in the garlic, cook for 1–2 minutes, then stir in the cream.

3. Let the mixture simmer gently for about 10 minutes, until the cream has reduced a bit and thickened, then season well with salt and pepper. Keep on one side until the pasta is done.

4. When the water boils, add the pasta to the pan, then let it bubble away, uncovered, for about 8 minutes or until it is *al dente*.

5. Just before the pasta is ready, gently reheat the sauce. Drain the pasta, return it to the still-warm saucepan and season with some salt, then add the sauce and most of the walnuts and stir so that all the pasta gets coated. Serve out on to warm plates with the remaining nuts sprinkled on top.
SERVES 2

TAGLIATELLE AL DOLCELATTE

Very quick and easy, this can be made with other blue cheeses, such as Gorgonzola, if you prefer. You can use light or heavy cream, depending on how rich you want it to be. A simple green salad, perhaps with some thin rings of red onion and a light balsamic vinegar vinaigrette, goes well with this.

3 ounces Dolcelatte
  cheese
⅔ cup light
  cream
1 tbs butter

salt and freshly
  ground black pepper
8 ounces tagliatelle
fresh Parmesan cheese,
  grated

1. First fill a saucepan with 2 quarts of water and bring to the boil for the pasta.

2. Next start making the sauce: crumble the Dolcelatte into a saucepan and add the cream and butter. Heat gently, stirring, until the ingredients have melted together and formed a sauce. Remove from the heat and season with salt and pepper.

3. When the water boils, add the pasta to the pan, then let it bubble away, uncovered, for about 8 minutes or until it is *al dente*.

4. Just before the pasta is ready, gently reheat the sauce. Drain the pasta, return it to the still-warm saucepan and season with some salt; then add the sauce and stir so that all the pasta gets coated. Serve out on to warm plates and hand round the Parmesan separately.
SERVES 2

PAPPARDELLE WITH CREAM AND PARMESAN

This delicious and simple pasta dish is rich, but can be enjoyed as part of a healthy diet if you serve it as a main course with a simple salad of leaves or ripe plum tomatoes and keep the rest of the day's meals free from fat: balance is the key. I love this made with wide ribbon pasta – pappardelle – but you could use a lighter, finer ribbon type such as tagliatelle or fettuccine, if you prefer. Really good freshly grated Parmesan cheese makes all the difference to this recipe.

6–8 ounces pappardelle	*salt and freshly ground black pepper*
2 tbs butter	*⅔ cup grated Parmesan cheese*
⅔ cup heavy cream	

1 Fill a saucepan with 2 quarts of water and bring to the boil. Add the pasta and cook uncovered, for about 8 minutes, until it is *al dente*.

2 Just before the pasta is ready, put the butter and cream into a small saucepan and heat gently until the butter has melted into the cream.

3 Drain the pasta, return it to the still-warm saucepan and season with salt. Pour in the cream mixture and add the Parmesan cheese. Check the seasoning, adding plenty of freshly ground black pepper, then serve at once on to warmed plates.

SERVES 2

FARFALLE WITH NO-COOK MASCARPONE SAUCE

Another almost-instant pasta dish, which you can flavor in any way you please – try chopped fresh herbs, crushed garlic, sun-dried tomatoes, or simply lots of coarsely ground black pepper. It's quite rich, so a refreshing salad – tomato and basil is my favorite – is all the accompaniment it needs.

8 ounces farfalle	*salt and freshly ground black pepper*
½ cup mascarpone cheese	*fresh Parmesan cheese (optional)*
freshly grated nutmeg	

1 Fill a saucepan with 2 quarts of water and bring to the boil. Add the pasta then cook, uncovered, for about 8 minutes, until it is *al dente*.

2 Drain the pasta then put it back into the pan. Add the mascarpone and some nutmeg and mix gently. Season well, then serve topped with some flaked or freshly grated Parmesan if you wish.

SERVES 2

CONCHIGLIE WITH RICOTTA AND SPINACH

6 ounces conchiglie	*salt and freshly ground black pepper*
8 ounces tender fresh spinach or frozen leaf spinach	*freshly grated nutmeg*
1 tbs olive oil	*fresh Parmesan cheese, grated*
1 garlic clove, crushed	
½ cup ricotta cheese	

1 First fill a saucepan with 2 quarts of water and bring to the boil. Add the pasta and cook, uncovered, for about 8 minutes, or until *al dente*.

2 If you're using fresh spinach, wash it in two or three changes of water, removing any tough stalks.

3 Heat the oil in a saucepan and put in the garlic. Cook for a few seconds, then add the spinach and cook over a high heat until the spinach has wilted and is tender. If the frozen spinach is very solid it will take a bit longer and you will need to watch it carefully to make sure it doesn't stick.

4 Drain the conchiglie, return it to the pan and gently stir in the spinach and the ricotta. Season with salt, pepper and freshly grated nutmeg and serve at once, with Parmesan cheese.

SERVES 2

Small pasta shapes work best for this recipe – farfalle, fusilli or lumache, for instance.

65

MACARONI AND CHEESE

Macaroni and cheese is so popular with my daughter Claire and her friends that I get tired of making it, though they never seem to get tired of eating it. I try to vary it by adding different ingredients. In this version tomatoes add freshness and moisture as well as color. I would serve it with watercress or, for the children, probably frozen peas (and ketchup!).

¾ cup quick-cooking elbow macaroni	FOR THE CHEESE SAUCE
	2 tbs butter
1 or 2 medium to large tomatoes	¼ cup flour
	1¼ cups skim milk
breadcrumbs made from 1 small slice of stale bread	½ tsp mustard powder
	3 tbs finely grated Parmesan cheese
1 tbs finely grated Parmesan cheese	salt and freshly ground black pepper

1 Bring a large saucepan of water to the boil, add the macaroni then cook, uncovered, for about 8 minutes or until the macaroni is *al dente*.

2 Meanwhile, make the cheese sauce: melt the butter in a saucepan and stir in the flour. When it froths, stir in about a third of the milk then beat well, over the heat, until it thickens. Repeat until all the milk has been used. Don't worry if it goes lumpy; just keep beating and all will be well.

3 Let the sauce simmer gently for a few minutes. Blend the mustard powder with a little water and add to the sauce, with the cheese and seasoning.

4 Heat the broiler. When the macaroni is done, drain and add to the sauce. Check the seasoning, adding more salt and pepper if necessary.

5 Slice the tomatoes. Put the macaroni and cheese into a shallow heatproof dish then cover with the tomato slices. Top with a light scattering of breadcrumbs and the cheese. Broil for a few minutes until the topping is golden brown.

SERVES 2

OPPOSITE: *(top) Fettuccine with Asparagus Sauce and (bottom) Macaroni and Cheese*

FETTUCCINE WITH ASPARAGUS SAUCE

This is a lovely summery pasta dish; a salad of lettuce and fresh herbs goes well with it.

1 tbs butter	salt and freshly ground black pepper
1 onion, peeled and chopped	freshly grated nutmeg
1 garlic clove, crushed	4–8 ounces asparagus spears
⅔ cup heavy cream	8 ounces fettuccine

1 First fill a saucepan with 2 quarts of water and bring to the boil for the pasta.

2 Next start making the sauce: melt the butter in a small saucepan then put in the onion, cover and cook gently for 10 minutes, until tender but not brown. Stir in the garlic, cook for 1–2 minutes, then stir in the cream. Let the mixture simmer gently for about 10 minutes, until the cream has reduced a bit and thickened. Season with salt, pepper and freshly grated nutmeg and keep on one side until the pasta is done.

3 While the sauce is cooking, trim the asparagus, removing the ends of the stems if they are tough and cutting it into 1-inch lengths. Keep the tips separate from the stems.

4 Bring 1 inch of water to the boil in a pan and put in the chopped asparagus stems. Boil for 2 minutes, then add the tips, cover and cook for a further 2 minutes, or until they are beginning to get tender but are still crunchy. Drain well, then stir into the cream sauce, reserving a few of the asparagus tips.

5 When the water boils, add the pasta to the pan, and let it bubble away, uncovered, for about 8 minutes or until it is *al dente*.

6 Just before the pasta is ready, gently reheat the sauce. Drain the pasta, return it to the still-warm saucepan and season with some salt; then add the sauce and stir so that all the pasta gets coated.

7 Serve out on to warm plates with the reserved asparagus tips on top, and grind on some additional coarse black pepper if liked.

SERVES 2

TAGLIATELLE WITH INSTANT GARLIC AND CHEESE SAUCE

8 ounces tagliatelle
½ cup Boursin cheese

salt and freshly
ground black pepper

1 Fill a saucepan with 2 quarts of water and bring to the boil then add the pasta and cook, uncovered, for about 8 minutes, until it is *al dente*.
2 Drain the pasta then put it back in the pan. Gently mix in the cheese, season well, then serve out on to warmed plates.
SERVES 2

FUSILLI WITH LEMON, CREAM AND PEAS

I think of this as a summer recipe, but it's also lovely in the winter, bringing a feeling of sunshine with it.

1 tbs butter
1 onion, peeled and
  chopped
1 garlic clove, crushed
⅔ cup heavy or light
  cream
grated rind of ½ lemon

salt and freshly
  ground black pepper
6 ounces fusilli or
  rotini
1 cup fresh shelled
  peas, or frozen peas
6 basil leaves

1 First fill a saucepan with 2 quarts of water and bring to the boil for the pasta.
2 Meanwhile, melt the butter in a pan then put in the onion, cover and cook for 10 minutes, until tender but not brown. Stir in the garlic and cook for 1–2 minutes longer, then stir in the cream and simmer gently for 10 minutes, until it has reduced a bit and thickened. Add the lemon rind and seasoning.
3 When the water boils, add the pasta to the pan, and cook, uncovered, for 8 minutes, until *al dente*.
4 Cook the peas in a little boiling water for 2–3 minutes or until they are just tender, then drain.

5 Just before the pasta is ready, gently reheat the sauce and add the peas. Drain the pasta, return it to the pan and add some salt, then stir in the sauce. Tear in the basil leaves, stir again, then serve.
SERVES 2

CONCHIGLIE WITH ZUCCHINI AND CREAM

1 tbs butter
1 onion, peeled and
  chopped
1 garlic clove, crushed
⅔ cup heavy or light
  cream
salt and freshly
  ground black pepper

6 ounces conchiglie
8 ounces zucchini
small bunch of chervil
  or parsley
lemon juice

1 First fill a saucepan with 2 quarts of water and bring to the boil for the pasta.
2 Meanwhile, melt the butter in a pan then put in the onion, cover and cook gently for 10 minutes, until tender but not brown. Add the garlic and cook for 1–2 minutes longer, then stir in the cream and simmer gently for about 10 minutes, until it has reduced a bit and thickened. Season to taste.
3 When the water boils, add the pasta to the pan and cook, uncovered, for 8 minutes, until *al dente*.
4 Slice the zucchini then cook them in a little boiling water for about 2 minutes, until just tender but still slightly crisp. Drain and add to the sauce.
5 Wash and chop the chervil or parsley – you need about 2 tablespoons.
6 Just before the pasta is ready, gently reheat the sauce. Drain the pasta, return it to the pan and add some salt; then stir in the sauce and the herbs. Add a little lemon juice to sharpen the sauce then serve out on to warmed plates.
SERVES 2

FARFALLE WITH CREAMY BROCCOLI SAUCE

The cream sauce in this case is a Béchamel. For a lighter version, you can leave out the cream and use skim milk instead of regular milk.

2 tbs butter	6 ounces farfalle
2 tbs flour	8 ounces broccoli
1¼ cups milk	salt and freshly
1 bay leaf	ground black pepper
a few stalks of	4 tbs cream (optional)
parsley, if available	freshly grated nutmeg
slice of onion, if	
available	

1 First fill a saucepan with 2 quarts of water and bring to the boil for the pasta.

2 Meanwhile, make the sauce: melt the butter in a saucepan and stir in the flour. When it froths, stir in half the milk and beat well, over the heat, until it thickens, then stir in the rest of the milk and keep stirring vigorously over the heat until the sauce is thick and smooth. Add the bay leaf, along with the parsley stalks and slice of onion if you have them, then contine to cook the sauce over a very low heat.

3 When the water boils, add the pasta then let it bubble away, uncovered, for about 8 minutes, until it is *al dente*.

4 Wash the broccoli then break or chop the flow-erets into bite-sized pieces and peel and slice into matchsticks any of the stalk that is tender enough to use. Cook the broccoli in 2 inches of boiling water for 3–4 minutes, until it is just tender. Drain and keep it warm.

5 Drain the pasta and return it to the saucepan. Add the broccoli and season with some salt. Remove the bay leaf, onion and parsley from the sauce, scraping as much sauce off them as you can, then discard them. If you're using the cream, stir this into the sauce over the heat, and season with salt, pepper and freshly grated nutmeg to taste.

6 Pour the sauce in with the pasta and broccoli, stir gently to mix, then serve.

SERVES 2

FETTUCCINE WITH CREAM AND HERB SAUCE

This sauce can be made with either light or heavy cream, depending on how rich you want it to be. (It's most delicious with heavy cream, I have to say, but it does work with light cream.) You can use almost any fresh herbs: I like chervil, parsley and chives, or tarragon for a more assertive flavor.

1 tbs butter	salt and freshly
1 onion, peeled and	ground black pepper
chopped	freshly grated nutmeg
1 garlic clove, crushed	bunch of mixed fresh
⅔ cup heavy or light	herbs
cream	8 ounces fettuccine

1 First fill a saucepan with 2 quarts of water and bring to the boil for the pasta.

2 Next start making the sauce: melt the butter in a small saucepan then put in the onion, cover and cook gently for 10 minutes, until tender but not brown. Add the garlic and cook for 1–2 minutes longer, then stir in the cream and leave the mixture to simmer gently for about 10 minutes, until the cream has reduced a bit and thickened. Season with salt, pepper and freshly grated nutmeg and keep on one side until the pasta is done.

3 While the sauce is cooking, wash and chop the herbs – you need about 2–4 tablespoons.

4 When the water boils, add the fettuccine to the pan and let it bubble away, uncovered, for about 8 minutes or until it is *al dente*.

5 Just before the pasta is ready, gently reheat the sauce. Drain the fettuccine, return it to the still-warm saucepan and season with some salt; then add the sauce and most of the herbs and stir so that all the pasta gets coated. Serve out on to warm plates with the remaining herbs scattered on top.

SERVES 2

Freshly grated nutmeg is a useful flavoring: buy a nutmeg grater and some whole nutmegs – they can be grated in moments.

LEGUMES, GRAINS & NUTS

These are packed full of nutrients. Nuts are a very concentrated source of energy, and small quantities go a long way. They make a wonderful fast food – great for putting into lunchboxes with some salad or fruit for a nourishing, fastest-ever meal. Most legumes need soaking and long cooking, so all the recipes in this book rely on canned ones to save time, except for red lentils which cook quickly without soaking. Grains are invaluable, too, and are much richer in protein, minerals and vitamins than many people realize.

BEANS & LENTILS
✳

CHICK PEA BROTH WITH PARSLEY DUMPLINGS

This is cheap, comforting, tasty and quick to make: what more can one ask of a simple recipe? The dumplings are based on one of Nigel Slater's recipes.

A few drops of lemon juice, added at the end of cooking, perk up many dishes in a magical way. But it must be freshly squeezed—other types don't have the same effect. Any leftover juice can be frozen in an ice-cube container.

2 onions
4 garlic cloves
4 carrots
4 celery stalks
2 tbs oil
3½ cups canned chick peas
salt and freshly ground black pepper

FOR THE DUMPLINGS
1¾ cups flour
2 tsp baking powder
1 tsp salt
½ cup grated Cheddar cheese
4–6 tbs chopped fresh parsley
1 egg
about ½ cup milk

1 Peel and chop the onions; peel and crush the garlic; scrape the carrots and cut them into thin rounds; trim and dice the celery. The vegetables need to be cut up small so that they will cook quickly.

2 Heat the oil in a large saucepan and cook the vegetables, with a lid on the pan, for 5 minutes. Then add the chick peas, together with their liquid, 7½ cups of water and some salt and pepper. Cover and leave to simmer for 15–20 minutes.

3 Meanwhile, make the dumplings: sift the flour and baking powder into a bowl and add the salt, grated cheese and parsley. Whisk the egg and stir that in, along with enough milk to make a soft but not sticky dough. Form the dough into eight balls and drop these into the soup.

4 Cover the pan and leave to cook for 10–12 minutes, until the dumplings are puffed up, light and cooked through, and all the vegetables are tender.
SERVES 4

TUSCAN BEAN SOUP

This soup makes a good light meal on its own with some bread, or serve it with some crostini (see pages 12–14) and a chunky Bibb lettuce salad for a more substantial meal.

1 tbs olive oil
1 onion, peeled and chopped
2 garlic cloves, crushed
1¾ cups canned cannellini beans

salt and freshly ground black pepper
lemon juice
extra virgin olive oil (optional)
roughly chopped flat-leaf parsley

1 Heat the oil in a large saucepan, add the onion then cover and cook gently for 10 minutes, until tender but not brown. Stir in the garlic and cook for 1–2 minutes longer.

2 Add the cannellini beans, together with their liquid, then purée in a food processor or blender until fairly smooth and creamy.

3 Return the mixture to the pan and add some water to adjust the consistency to your liking: about 1¼ cups makes a medium-thick soup. Bring to the boil then season with salt and pepper and a squeeze or two of lemon juice.

4 Serve the soup in warmed bowls, topped with some extra virgin olive oil, if you like, some flat-leaf parsley and coarsely ground black pepper.
SERVES 2

SPICY LENTIL SOUP

1 tbs oil	*pinch of chili powder*
1 onion, peeled and	*1 bay leaf*
chopped	*1 cup split red lentils*
8–10 cardamom pods	*juice of ½–1 lemon*
2 garlic cloves,	*salt and freshly*
crushed	*ground black pepper*
1½ tsp turmeric	

1 Heat the oil in a large saucepan, then add the onion, cover and cook gently for 5–7 minutes.

2 Meanwhile, bruise the cardamom pods in a pestle and mortar or with a wooden spoon. Add them to the onion, along with the garlic, turmeric, chili powder and bay leaf, and cook over a gentle heat for a further 2–3 minutes.

3 Stir in the lentils, then pour in 4 cups of water. Bring to the boil and simmer, uncovered, for 20–25 minutes, until the lentils are very tender and pale colored.

4 Sharpen the flavor with lemon juice to taste, season with salt and pepper and then serve, accompanied by poppadums if you like.

SERVES 2

LIMA BEAN AND TOMATO SOUP

Lima bean and tomato is a combination I remember from my vegetarian childhood and I still think it's good. Cheesy garlic bread or bruschetta (see pages 12–14) go well with it.

1 tbs olive oil or oil	*1¾ cups canned lima*
from a jar of	*beans*
sun-dried tomatoes	*3–4 sun-dried*
1 onion, peeled and	*tomatoes*
chopped	*salt and freshly*
1 garlic clove, crushed	*ground black pepper*
1¾ cups canned	
tomatoes	

1 Heat the oil in a large saucepan then add the onion, cover and cook gently for 5 minutes, until softened. Stir in the garlic and cook for 2 minutes, then pour in the canned tomatoes and the lima beans, together with their liquid.

2 Chop the sun-dried tomatoes and add these to the pan. Simmer, uncovered, for about 10 minutes.

3 You can serve the soup as it is, but I think it's nicest if you purée half of it in a food processor or blender then stir it back in, because this gives a slightly thickened, creamy consistency. Season with salt and pepper and serve.

SERVES 2

PROVENCAL FLAGEOLET SOUP

This is light yet filling, and the pesto gives it a sunny Mediterranean flavor. It's good with some warm multigrain bread or hot garlic bread.

1 large carrot	*1 garlic clove, crushed*
1 tbs olive oil	*1¾ cups canned*
1 onion, peeled and	*flageolets*
chopped	*1–2 tbs pesto*
1 large leek	*salt and freshly*
2 small zucchini	*ground black pepper*

1 Scrape the carrot then cut it into tiny dice (about ¼ inch) so that it will cook quickly. Heat the oil in a large saucepan and fry the onion and carrot, with a lid on the pan, for 5 minutes, until beginning to soften. Wash, trim and finely slice the leek; wash, trim and dice the zucchini.

2 Add the leek and the garlic to the pan; cover and cook for a further 5 minutes, then add the zucchini, flageolets and 2½ cups of water. Bring to the boil and simmer for about 10 minutes until the vegetables are tender.

3 Stir in pesto to taste and season with salt and pepper, then serve.

SERVES 2

LENTIL CHILI BURGERS WITH DILL SAUCE

This is a pleasant combination of hot and cool, crisp and creamy. Serve with a simple salad or a steamed vegetable such as broccoli. The burgers are nicest if they are deep-fried, which you can do quickly in a medium saucepan rather than going through all the rigmarole of getting out a deep-fat fryer – or they can be shallow-fried.

1 onion, peeled and chopped	**1 bunch of fresh cilantro, chopped**
1 tbs olive oil	**salt and freshly ground black pepper**
1 garlic clove, crushed	
1 fresh green chili, de-seeded and chopped, or chili powder to taste	**1 egg, beaten**
	4 tbs dry breadcrumbs
2 tsp ground coriander	
1¾ cups canned green lentils, drained	**FOR THE SAUCE**
	2–3 tbs chopped fresh dill
oil for deep- or shallow-frying	**⅔ cup creamy yogurt**
1 slice of white or whole wheat bread, crusts removed	

1. Fry the onion in the oil, with a lid on the pan, for 5 minutes. Add the garlic, chili and ground coriander, then cover and cook for 2–3 minutes. Remove from the heat and stir in the lentils.

2. If you are going to deep-fry the burgers, put the oil on to heat, but keep your eye on it. Cover the bread with water, drain immediately, then squeeze out all the water and crumble the bread – this is a quick way of making breadcrumbs. Add to the lentil mixture along with the fresh cilantro and seasoning, mashing the mixture with the spoon or a potato masher so that it holds together.

3. Divide the mixture into four and form into sphere shapes if you are going to deep-fry them, or flattish burger shapes for shallow-frying.

4. Dip the burgers first in the beaten egg, then in the dry breadcrumbs, making sure they are well coated. Then fry them until crisp and brown: they will need about 3–4 minutes on each side if shallow-frying and 4–5 minutes in total if deep-frying. Drain them well on paper towels.

5. Serve with a sauce made by stirring the chopped dill into the creamy yogurt and seasoning with salt and pepper.

SERVES 2

LENTILS WITH ROASTED BELL PEPPERS

This is a very pleasant combination of flavors, textures and colors: so simple, but so good. I like a green salad with it and some good light bread, such as ciabatta.

1 large red bell pepper	**2 tbs balsamic vinegar**
1 large yellow bell pepper	**salt and freshly ground black pepper**
1¾ cups canned green or brown lentils	
	sprigs of basil

1. Cut the bell peppers into quarters, place them cut-side down on a broiler pan and broil them on high for 10 minutes or until the skins have blistered and charred in places. Remove from the broiler and cover with a damp cloth.

2. Meanwhile, gently heat the lentils, in their liquid, in a saucepan.

3. When the bell peppers are cool enough to handle, pull off the skin with a sharp knife, discard the seeds and stalks, cut the flesh into strips and put into a serving dish.

4. Drain the lentils and add to the peppers with the balsamic vinegar, salt and pepper to taste, and some torn basil leaves.

SERVES 2

OPPOSITE: *(left) Lentil Chili Burgers with Dill Sauce, (above) Provençal Flageolet Soup, page 73, (right) Lentils with Roasted Bell Peppers*

LENTILS WITH CORIANDER AND HARD-COOKED EGGS

Hard-cooked eggs and lentils are one of those classic combinations, like tomato and basil or bread and cheese – and a colorful and nutritious pair they are too. Serve this on its own or with some rice, bread or chutney – it's very versatile, so please yourself!

If you can get the little Puy lentils, which cook in 40 minutes, you can use them for this recipe instead of canned green lentils. Cook them in plenty of boiling water until tender.

2 eggs
1 tbs olive oil
1 onion, peeled and sliced
1 garlic clove, crushed
2 tsp ground coriander

1¾ cups canned green lentils, drained
2 tbs chopped fresh cilantro
salt and freshly ground black pepper

1 Hard-cook the eggs by simmering them in a pan of boiling water for 7–10 minutes. Then drain them, cover with cold water and leave to cool.

2 Heat the olive oil in a pan, add the onion and garlic then cover and cook gently for 5 minutes, until softened.

3 Add the ground coriander to the onion and garlic, stirring for 1–2 minutes, then put in the lentils and leave to cook very gently until the lentils are thoroughly heated. Meanwhile, peel the hard-cooked eggs, rinse them under cold water, then slice them.

4 Add the chopped fresh cilantro to the lentil mixture, taste and season with salt and pepper. Serve the lentils and the eggs together: you could stir the eggs into the lentil mixture if you wish, or just arrange them around it attractively.

SERVES 2

CHICK PEA CROQUETTES WITH CILANTRO RAITA

These are crisp on the outside, moist and spicy within, lovely with a yogurt raita and a fresh salad – perhaps diced cucumber and chopped scallions. You really do need a food processor to purée the chick peas for this recipe.

1 onion, peeled and chopped
1 tbs olive oil
1 garlic clove, crushed
1 tsp cumin seeds
1¾ cups canned chick peas, drained
salt and freshly ground black pepper
1 egg, beaten

4 tbs dry breadcrumbs
oil for shallow-frying

FOR THE RAITA
2 tbs chopped fresh cilantro
⅔ cup creamy yogurt

1 Fry the onion in the oil, with a lid on the pan, for 5 minutes, until beginning to soften, then add the garlic and cumin seeds and fry for a further 2–3 minutes. Remove from the heat.

2 Put the onion mixture into a food processor. Drain the chick peas, reserving the liquid, then add them to the food processor and whizz to form a thick purée that holds together. If necessary, add a little of the reserved chick pea liquid to obtain the right consistency, but be careful not to let the mixture get too moist.

3 Season with salt and pepper, then divide the mixture into four and form into flattish croquettes; don't make them too thick or the inside won't heat through properly.

4 Dip the croquettes first in the beaten egg then in the dry breadcrumbs, making sure they are well coated. Then heat the oil in a skillet and shallow-fry the croquettes for 3–4 minutes on each side, until crisp and brown. Drain them well on paper towels.

5 Serve with a raita made by stirring the chopped cilantro into the creamy yogurt and seasoning with salt and pepper.

SERVES 2

CHICK PEA PUREE WITH SPICED ONION TOPPING

This is so simple to make, and good with some warm bread and perhaps a cucumber and tomato salad with some chopped fresh cilantro and slices of lemon.

2 onions, peeled and
  chopped
2 tbs olive oil
2 garlic cloves,
  crushed
2 tsp ground coriander

1 tsp ground cumin
1¾ cups canned chick
  peas
salt and freshly
  ground black pepper

1. Fry the onions in the oil, with a lid on the pan, for 5 minutes or until beginning to soften, then add the garlic, coriander and cumin.

2. Cover and fry for a further 2–3 minutes, then take out a third of the mixture and put it into a food processor. Continue to cook the rest of the onions and spices until the onions are brown, but don't have the heat too high or the spices might burn.

3. Meanwhile, put the chick peas and about half of their liquid into the food processor with the onions. Whizz to a purée, adding more of the liquid if necessary to make a thick but creamy mixture.

4. Season with salt and pepper, then transfer the purée to a pan and heat through. Serve topped with the crisp, browned spicy onion mixture.

SERVES 2

RED BEAN BURGERS WITH SOUR CREAM SAUCE

Sour cream has the same fat content as light cream, so it's not over-rich when used in small quantities. However, for a lower-fat sauce plain yogurt is very good instead. Another option is to serve the burgers with a good dollop of guacamole (see page 21) or, of course, you could forget about a sauce altogether and serve the burgers in light rolls or with salad.

1 onion, peeled and
  chopped
1 tbs olive oil
1 garlic clove, crushed
1 tomato
4 slices of bread,
  crusts removed
1¾ cups canned red
  kidney beans,
  drained
salt and freshly
  ground black pepper

1 egg, beaten
4 tbs dry
  breadcrumbs
oil for shallow-frying

FOR THE SAUCE
2 tbs snipped fresh
  chives
⅔ cup sour cream

1. Fry the onion in the oil, with a lid on the pan, for 5 minutes, until beginning to soften. Add the garlic and fry for a further 2–3 minutes.

2. Meanwhile, pour boiling water over the tomato and leave for a few seconds until the skin splits, then slip off the skin with a sharp knife. De-seed and chop the tomato, removing any hard bits of core, then add it to the onion and garlic. Stir, then cook, uncovered for 3–4 minutes, until the tomato has cooked down a bit.

3. Remove the pan from the heat. Roughly tear the bread and add to the pan, together with the beans. The mixture has to be mashed very well at this stage to blend together all the ingredients, and the easiest way to do this is to tip it into a food processor and whizz it to a thick purée. You can do it by hand, however, with plenty of patience and a good strong potato masher.

4. Season the mixture with salt and pepper, then divide it into four and form into flattish burger shapes; don't make them too thick or the inside won't heat through.

5. Dip the burgers first in the beaten egg then in the dry breadcrumbs, making sure they are well coated. Then heat the oil in a skillet and shallow-fry them for 3–4 minutes on each side, until they are crisp and brown. Drain them well on paper towels.

6. Serve the burgers straight away with a sauce made by stirring the snipped fresh chives into the sour cream and seasoning with salt and pepper to taste.

SERVES 2

Cumin (both whole and ground) and coriander (ground is most useful) are wonderful for flavoring legumes and vegetables.

ULTIMATE RED BEAN CHILI

This quick chili is good with bread, mashed potatoes, plain pasta or rice, or some potato wedges, sour cream and chives (see page 106). If there is any left over, it's nice cold as a salad, or stuffed into pita bread, or as a filling for crêpes or tortillas.

1 tbs olive oil	*1 large green chili*
1 onion, peeled and chopped	*1¾ cups canned red kidney beans, drained*
1 red bell pepper	*salt and freshly ground black pepper*
1 large carrot	*ground black pepper*
1 garlic clove, crushed	*chili powder (optional)*
1¾ cups canned tomatoes	

1️⃣ Heat the oil in a medium-large saucepan, then put in the onion, cover and cook for 5 minutes.

2️⃣ De-seed and chop the red bell pepper; scrape and dice the carrot. Add to the pan with the garlic. Stir, then cover and cook for 10 minutes.

3️⃣ Stir the tomatoes into the mixture, breaking them up with the spoon. De-seed the chili, slice it into rings and add it to the saucepan. Cook gently, uncovered, for 10–15 minutes or until the carrot is tender.

4️⃣ Put in the red kidney beans and cook for a further 1–2 minutes to heat them through. Season with salt and pepper and add a pinch or so of chili powder if it needs more of a kick, then serve.

SERVES 2

RED BEANS WITH THYME AND COCONUT CREAM

This is a quick version of a West Indian recipe. It's very warming and good with some rice. I think brown rice goes best with it, but if you're doing that you'll need to get it started first to give it time to cook.

⅔ cup unsweetened shredded coconut	*1 carrot, finely sliced*
1¾ cups canned red kidney beans	*1 garlic clove, crushed*
1 onion, peeled and chopped	*1 tsp dried thyme or 1 tbs fresh thyme*
	salt and freshly ground black pepper

1️⃣ Put the coconut in a bowl, pour over 1¼ cups of boiling water and leave to steep for 5 minutes.

2️⃣ Strain, pressing as much liquid out of the coconut as possible, discard the coconut, and put the liquid in a pan with the red kidney beans.

3️⃣ Add the onion, carrot, garlic and thyme and simmer gently for about 15 minutes, until the vegetables are tender. Then season and serve.

SERVES 2

TWO-BEAN SALAD WITH GARLIC BREAD

3½ cups canned beans; use a mixture of 2 contrasting types	*salt and freshly ground black pepper*
1–2 tsp balsamic vinegar	*2–4 tbs chopped fresh herbs, such as chives, parsley and chervil or tarragon*
3 tbs olive oil or plain yogurt, or a mixture	*few thin slices of red onion (optional)*
½ tsp Dijon mustard (optional)	*garlic bread (see page 28)*

1️⃣ Drain the beans. Mix 1 teaspoon of balsamic vinegar with the oil and/or yogurt in a salad bowl. Taste, and add more vinegar if necessary. Add the mustard, if you're using this, and plenty of seasoning.

2️⃣ Add the beans, herbs and onion, if you're using this; stir gently then leave on one side while you prepare the garlic bread. Stir again before serving.

SERVES 4

OPPOSITE: *Ultimate Red Bean Chili*

This is a very easy salad which can be varied as much as you like by using different dressings, different types of beans and additional ingredients. Hot garlic bread goes well with it. Any leftover salad will keep well for 24 hours, covered, in the fridge.

MEXICAN BEAN SALAD

1 small lettuce
4 tomatoes
1 small red bell pepper
1 tbs olive oil
1 onion, peeled and
   chopped
1 green chili
1 garlic clove, crushed
1¾ cups canned red
   kidney beans,
   drained

salt and freshly
   ground black pepper
1 avocado
2 tbs snipped fresh
   chives
⅔ cup plain low-fat
   yogurt or sour cream
a few fresh cilantro
   leaves, if available

1 Wash the lettuce and put it into a colander to drain. Put the tomatoes in a bowl, pour boiling water over them and leave for a few seconds until the skins split. Drain, cover with cold water and slip off the skins. Cut two of the tomatoes into eighths and chop the other two. Wash and slice the bell pepper, discarding the stalk and seeds.

2 Heat the oil in a saucepan then add the onion; cover and cook over a moderate heat for 5 minutes, stirring occasionally.

3 Meanwhile, de-seed and chop the chili, washing your hands carefully after handling it. Add the chili, garlic and chopped tomatoes to the onion and cook for 5 minutes.

4 Add the beans to the onion mixture, mashing them roughly with a wooden spoon or a potato masher to give a chunky texture. Heat through, then season with salt and pepper and keep warm over a low heat.

5 Cover a large platter with the lettuce leaves and arrange the red pepper and tomato randomly on top.

6 Peel, pit and roughly chop the avocado. Stir the chives into the yogurt or sour cream.

7 Spoon the red bean mixture on to the center of the salad. Sprinkle the chopped avocado over it, then drizzle some of the yogurt or sour cream mixture over everything – put the rest into a small bowl to serve with the salad. Serve the salad at once, garnished with fresh cilantro leaves, if you have any.

SERVES 2

VARIATION

REFRIED BEANS WITH TORTILLA CHIPS

Omit the red bell pepper, 2 of the tomatoes and the avocado. Make the bean mixture as described above and stir some fresh cilantro into it, if available. Transfer to a shallow heatproof dish and top with a pack of tortilla chips and 1 cup of grated Cheddar cheese. Place under a hot broiler to melt the cheese, then serve with the lettuce leaves (crisp ones are best) and the yogurt or sour cream mixture.

WHITE BEANS COOKED IN CREAM

This is rich and delicious, lovely for a treat, with fingers of toast and a green salad.

1 tbs butter
1 onion, peeled and
   chopped
1 garlic clove, crushed
⅔ cup light cream
1¾ cups canned white
   beans, such as navy
   or cannellini
squeeze of lemon juice

salt and freshly
   ground black pepper
freshly grated nutmeg
fresh parsley

1 Melt the butter in a medium saucepan then put in the onion, cover and cook gently for 5 minutes, until tender but not brown.

2 Stir in the garlic and cook for 1–2 minutes longer, then stir in the cream and leave the mixture to simmer gently for about 5 minutes, until the cream has reduced a bit and thickened.

3 Drain the beans and add them to the pan. Heat gently, stirring often. Add the lemon juice and then season with salt, pepper and freshly grated nutmeg. Make sure the beans are really hot, then serve them out on to heated plates and snip a little parsley over the top.

SERVES 2

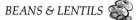

QUICK BEANY BAKE

There's nothing in the slightest bit gourmet about this recipe but it's adored by all kids. I think it originally came from a children's TV program – my daughter Kate told it to me.

1 tbs olive oil
1 onion, peeled and
  chopped
1 small can of baked
  beans
1 small can of red
  kidney beans,
  drained

1 cup canned corn
  kernels, drained
4–6 slices of bread
1 cup grated cheese

1 Heat the oil in a medium saucepan, then add the onion and cook, covered, for about 10 minutes, until it has softened.

2 Add the baked beans, kidney beans and corn kernels to the pan. Cook the mixture gently until everything is hot.

3 Heat the broiler. Transfer the beany mixture to a shallow heatproof dish that will fit under your broiler. Roughly tear the slices of bread over the top (with or without the crusts) then cover with the grated cheese.

4 Broil for about 10 minutes, or until the bread is crisp and the cheese melted and golden brown. Serve at once.

SERVES 2–4

EASY VEGETABLE DAL

Soothing and colorful, this is enough for two to four people depending on what you serve with it – Indian breads and/or boiled rice make good accompaniments. Any that's left over tastes good, if not better, the next day. This recipe contains no fat and is a special favorite of mine for that reason, as well as for its flavor and comforting qualities.

1 cup split red lentils
2 thin slices of fresh
  ginger root
½ tsp turmeric
1 tsp cumin seeds
1 tsp ground coriander
pinch of chili powder
1 onion

2 carrots
1 garlic clove
¾ cup frozen peas
juice of ½ lemon
salt and freshly
  ground black pepper

1 Put the lentils, ginger root, turmeric, cumin seeds, ground coriander and chili powder into a medium saucepan with 4 cups of water and bring to the boil.

2 Meanwhile, peel and slice the onion, scrape or peel the carrots and slice them quite finely, and peel and crush the garlic. Add all these vegetables to the lentils as they continue to simmer away. Let the lentil mixture cook for about 25 minutes altogether. At first it will look hopelessly watery, then when it is done it will become thick and soft, like porridge, and all the vegetables should be tender, too.

3 Add the peas to the mixture and cook for a further 2–3 minutes, until they are heated through. Then stir in the lemon juice and season to taste with salt and pepper.

SERVES 2–4

SPLIT PEA AND OKRA DAL

This quick dal uses canned split peas and is good served with poppadums, available from Indian food stores, and some basmati rice. I sometimes add sliced tomatoes and a coriander raita (see page 76) for an easy Indian meal. You can buy canned split peas from specialty health food stores. You could also use dried split peas for this recipe (although, obviously it won't be as fast): put 1 cup peas into a pan with three times their volume in water, bring to the boil and simmer gently until very tender – 40-50 minutes. Drain, then proceed as below.

1–2 tbs olive oil	½ tsp turmeric
2 onions, peeled and chopped	3½ cups canned yellow split peas
6 ounces okra	squeeze of lemon juice
1 green chili	salt and freshly ground black pepper
1 garlic clove, crushed	
2 tsp cumin seeds	chopped fresh cilantro (optional)
2 tsp ground coriander	

1 Heat the oil in a medium-large saucepan and put in the onions. Cook gently, with a lid on the pan, for 5 minutes.

2 Meanwhile, top and tail the okra and de-seed and chop the chili. Add these to the pan, along with the garlic, cook for 2–3 minutes, then put in the cumin seeds, ground coriander and turmeric and stir over the heat for a minute or two.

3 Add the split peas to the vegetables, together with their liquid, then cook gently, uncovered, for about 5–10 minutes or until the okra are tender and any wateriness has disappeared.

4 Add the lemon juice and salt and pepper to taste and serve sprinkled with chopped fresh cilantro, if you have it.

SERVES 4

OPPOSITE: *(left) Spiced Red Lentils and Potatoes with Caramelized Onions and (right) Split Pea and Okra Dal*

SPICED RED LENTILS AND POTATOES WITH CARAMELIZED ONIONS

This delicious spicy mixture evolved from the rather unpromising starting point of some potatoes and dried red lentils. It's good served with fresh chutney and a side salad.

⅓ cup unsweetened shredded coconut	½ tsp grated fresh ginger root
⅔ cup split red lentils	squeeze of lemon juice
8 ounces potatoes	3 tbs chopped fresh cilantro
2 onions, peeled and chopped	salt and freshly ground black pepper
1–2 tbs oil	paprika
1 garlic clove, crushed	
½ tsp turmeric	
½ tsp black mustard seeds	

1 Put the coconut into a bowl, pour over 2 cups of boiling water and leave to steep for 5 minutes. Then strain, pressing as much liquid out of the coconut as possible. Put the liquid in a pan, add the lentils and simmer, uncovered, for 20 minutes.

2 Meanwhile, peel the potatoes and cut them into 1-inch dice. Add these to the lentils after they have been cooking for 10 minutes. When the lentils are done – soft and pale-colored – the potatoes should be just tender. Remove from the heat.

3 Fry the onions in 1 tablespoon of oil, with a lid on the pan, for 5 minutes, then remove half the onion and put on one side for the moment. Stir the garlic, turmeric, mustard seeds and ginger into the remaining onion in the pan, cover and cook for a further 4–5 minutes.

4 Add the onion and spice mixture to the lentils and stir gently to combine. Then add the lemon juice, fresh cilantro and plenty of seasoning.

5 Put the remaining onion back in the pan, with more oil if necessary, and fry it over a moderate to high heat for 3–5 minutes, until golden brown and crisp. Serve the lentil mixture topped with the crisp onion and a sprinkling of paprika.

SERVES 2

To make fresh chutney to serve with this, mix together some chopped tomato, chopped red onion and plenty of chopped fresh mint; add a squeeze of lemon juice, a dash of balsamic vinegar and seasoning to taste.

RICE
— * —

SPICED VEGETABLE AND CASHEW PILAF

Although the ingredients list is quite long, this is actually very quick and easy to make. My favorite accompaniments are fresh chutney, mango chutney and Indian breads. I've given quantities to serve two, but for four just double everything except the oil. You can use brown or white basmati rice – white cooks more quickly.

2 tbs oil	1 cup basmati rice
1 onion, peeled and	small piece of
chopped	cinnamon stick
1 carrot, finely sliced	¼ tsp turmeric
1 leek, cleaned and	1 bay leaf
sliced	½ cup cashews
1 garlic clove, crushed	salt and freshly
6 cardamom pods	ground black pepper
1 tsp cumin seeds	

1 Heat the oil in a saucepan, then put in the onion and carrot, cover and cook for 5 minutes. Stir in the leek, garlic, cardamom and cumin, crushing the cardomom pods against the pan with a wooden spoon. Cover and cook for another 5–10 minutes, stirring occasionally, until the vegetables are tender.

2 Meanwhile, wash the rice in a strainer under cold running water, then put it into a saucepan with the cinnamon stick, turmeric, bay leaf and 2 cups of water. Bring to the boil, then cover, turn the heat right down and leave it to cook very gently for 10–12 minutes.

3 Heat the broiler. Spread out the cashews on a broiler pan and broil for 1–2 minutes, until they are golden brown, turning them to brown both sides. Remove from the broiler and leave on one side.

4 Fork the rice gently, then combine it with the vegetable mixture, stirring gently with the fork and adding some salt and pepper. Stir the cashews into the mixture just before you serve it.
SERVES 2

RICE WITH TOMATOES, CORN AND CHILI

The best rice to use for this is either ordinary white long grain rice or brown basmati, although you could use quick-cook brown long grain rice instead.

1 tbs oil	½ cup frozen corn
1 onion, peeled and	kernels
chopped	¾ cup frozen peas
1 fresh chili	salt and freshly ground
1 garlic clove, crushed	black pepper
1 cup rice	2 tbs chopped fresh
1 cup canned tomatoes	parsley
1 bay leaf	

1 Heat the oil in a large saucepan, then put in the onion, cover and cook for 5 minutes.

2 Halve, de-seed and chop the chili, being careful not to get the juice anywhere near your face, and washing your hands well afterwards. Add the chili and the garlic to the pan and stir well.

3 Add the rice, tomatoes, bay leaf and 2 cups of water to the pan. Bring to the boil, then turn down the heat, cover and leave to cook very gently for 20 minutes for brown basmati rice, 15–20 minutes for long grain white rice or 25 minutes for quick-cook brown rice.

4 Cook the frozen corn kernels and peas together in a little boiling water for 2 minutes then drain and add them to the rice mixture, along with some salt, pepper and the parsley. Stir gently with a fork and serve as soon as possible.
SERVES 2

WARM RICE SALAD

This looks fresh and pretty and is made with a delicious honey and garlic dressing; you can leave out the oil if you want a lighter result.

1 cup basmati rice
1 garlic clove, crushed
1 tbs honey
1 tbs vinegar
1 tbs olive oil
salt and freshly
  ground black pepper
8 ounces cherry
  tomatoes
4 tbs snipped fresh
  chives
4 tbs chopped fresh
  mint

1. Wash the rice in a strainer under cold running water, then put it into a saucepan with 2 cups of water. Bring to the boil, then cover, turn the heat right down and leave it to cook gently for 10–12 minutes. Turn off the heat and let the rice stand, covered, for a further 10 minutes, if there is time.

2. While the rice is cooking, make the dressing: put the garlic, honey, vinegar, olive oil and some salt and pepper into a large bowl and mix well.

3. Wash and slice the cherry tomatoes. Put the rice into the bowl with the dressing, add the cherry tomatoes and herbs then stir gently with a fork. Check the seasoning, then serve while still warm.

SERVES 2–3

EGG AND COCONUT CURRY

1 cup unsweetened
  shredded coconut
2 eggs
1 cup brown or white
  basmati rice
½ cinnamon stick
4 cloves
4 cardamom pods
salt and freshly
  ground black pepper
2 tbs butter
1 onion, peeled and
  chopped
1 garlic clove, crushed
2 tsp medium curry
  powder
¼ cup flour
2 tbs golden raisins
1 tbs lemon juice

1. Put the coconut in a bowl and cover with 2 cups of boiling water. Leave to infuse.

2. Hard-cook the eggs by simmering them in a pan of boiling water for 7–10 minutes. Then drain them, cover with cold water and leave to cool.

3. Wash the rice in a strainer under cold running water. Put it in a saucepan with 1½ cups of water, the cinnamon stick, cloves and cardamom, crushing the cardamom pods against the side of the pan with a wooden spoon. Add a good pinch of salt and bring to the boil.

4. Turn the heat down very low and leave the rice to cook until it is tender and all the water has been absorbed, 20 minutes for brown rice, 10–12 minutes for white rice. Then turn off the heat and leave it to stand, still covered, for 10 minutes.

5. Meanwhile, melt the butter in a pan and gently cook the onion and garlic for 5 minutes. Strain the coconut through a strainer, pressing it against the strainer to extract as much liquid as possible. Discard the coconut but keep the liquid.

6. Stir the curry powder into the onion mixture, then add the flour and stir for 1–2 minutes until it froths. Pour in the strained coconut water, stirring until it thickens. Add the golden raisins, then let it simmer very gently for 7–10 minutes.

7. Make sure the rice is still hot and check the seasoning; reheat it gently if necessary. Peel and slice the hard-cooked eggs and then add them to the sauce with the lemon juice and salt and pepper to taste. Fluff up the rice with a fork and serve with the curry.

SERVES 2

This is a simple English-style curry rather than an authentically spiced Indian one, and I think it makes a pleasant change. Using a medium curry powder will produce a mild curry here; you can adjust the heat according to the type and amount of curry powder you use.

VARIATIONS

1 CHEESE CURRY

Cut 4 ounces of cheese – haloumi if you want one that keeps its shape, or good old Cheddar for a 'melting' result – into smallish cubes and stir them into the sauce instead of the eggs. Heat gently until the cheese has warmed through, then serve.

2 LIMA BEAN OR SOYA BEAN CURRY

Add 1 cup of canned beans to the sauce instead of the eggs and cook gently until heated through.

ALL-SEASONS MUSHROOM RISOTTO

My favorite risotto is this rich-tasting mushroom one, with extra flavor coming from the porcini. Cremini mushrooms are good if you can get them, because they retain their firm texture and don't produce much liquid.

2 tbs dried porcini
   mushrooms
1 bay leaf
3 tbs olive oil
4 tbs butter
1 onion, peeled and
   chopped
12 ounces Cremini
   mushrooms or small
   white mushrooms
2 garlic cloves,
   crushed

2 cups Arborio or
   other risotto rice
salt and freshly
   ground black pepper
chopped fresh parsley,
   preferably flat-leaf
2 ounces fresh
   Parmesan cheese, cut
   into thin slivers

Although if pushed you can use an ordinary long grain rice, Arborio or risotto rice (which is now widely available) is best because it cooks to exactly the right creamy consistency, with the grains tender but slightly chewy.

1 Put the porcini into a saucepan with the bay leaf and 6 cups of boiling water. Let it simmer while you prepare the other ingredients.

2 Heat the olive oil and half the butter in a large saucepan, then put in the onion, cover and cook for about 5 minutes, until soft but not browned.

3 Slice the fresh mushrooms and add to the onion with the garlic and rice. Stir for 2–3 minutes, until the rice is coated with the buttery juices.

4 Add a ladleful of the simmering water from the pan containing the porcini and stir well; once it has been absorbed, add another. Keep the water in the porcini pan simmering away and continue to add it to the risotto a ladleful at a time as each addition is absorbed, stirring the risotto constantly.

5 Remove the porcini from the pan, chop them up and add them to the risotto. Stop adding water once the rice is tender but not soggy – *al dente*, in fact. This will be after about 20 minutes and you will probably have used all the water.

6 Stir in the rest of the butter and season to taste with salt and pepper. Serve immediately, scattered with the parsley and slivers of Parmesan.
SERVES 4

QUICK MICROWAVE RISOTTO

It's blissfully easy to make a risotto in the microwave and the results are wonderful. This method was developed by the food writer Barbara Kafka, and it works like a dream.

2 tbs butter
1 tbs olive oil
1 onion, peeled and
   chopped
3 garlic cloves,
   crushed

1 cup Arborio or other
   risotto rice
2 ounces fresh
   Parmesan cheese
salt and freshly
   ground black pepper

1 Put the butter and oil into a deep, microwave-proof pot, put into the microwave and cook, uncovered, on high for 2 minutes.

2 Add the onion and garlic and stir to coat them in the butter and oil. Cook, uncovered, on high, for 4 minutes.

3 Add the rice, stir, then cook, uncovered, on high for 4 minutes.

4 Pour in 3 cups of boiling water. Cook, uncovered, on high for 9 minutes. Stir well, then cook for 9 minutes more.

5 Remove from the microwave. Let the risotto stand, uncovered, for 5 minutes, so the rice absorbs the rest of the liquid; stir it several times. Flake the Parmesan with a vegetable parer or a sharp knife then stir this in, together with salt and pepper to taste. Serve immediately.
SERVES 2

OPPOSITE: *All-Seasons Mushroom Risotto*

87

BULGUR, COUSCOUS & POLENTA

BULGUR AND CHEESE PILAF

Bulgur wheat is crushed and pre-cooked so it is quick to prepare. You can serve it as a side dish, like rice, or you can stir in some extra ingredients and turn it into a main course, as in this recipe.

1 tbs olive oil	*salt and freshly*
1 tbs butter	*ground black pepper*
1 onion, peeled and	*⅓ cup almonds*
chopped	*4 ounces Gruyère*
1 red bell pepper, de-	*cheese*
seeded and chopped	*2 tbs chopped fresh*
2 garlic cloves,	*parsley*
crushed	
1¼ cups bulgur wheat	
⅓ cup raisins	

Serve this pilaf with a salad of green leaves, herbs, a little finely sliced onion, and a light lemon and olive oil dressing. A sour cream sauce is a luxurious finishing touch (see page 77).

1 Heat the oil and butter in a large saucepan and put in the onion and red bell pepper; stir, then cover and leave to cook gently for 5–10 minutes. Add the garlic and cook for a few minutes longer.

2 Add the bulgur wheat and raisins to the onion and pepper mixture, stirring well so that the wheat gets coated with the butter and oil, then pour in 2½ cups of boiling water and add a good teaspoonful of salt. Bring to the boil, then cover and leave to cook gently for 15 minutes.

3 Meanwhile put the almonds into a small saucepan, cover with water and bring to the boil. Boil for 1–2 minutes, then drain and slip off the skins with your fingers.

4 Heat the broiler. Cut the almonds lengthwise with a sharp knife to make long slivers. Spread these out on a broiler pan and broil them for 1–2 minutes, until golden brown.

5 Cut the Gruyère cheese into ½-inch dice. Add it to the bulgur wheat, together with the almonds and parsley, forking them through gently. Check the seasoning, then serve.

SERVES 4

BRIGHTLY COLORED TABBOULEH

Here's a deliciously inauthentic version of this famous salad: it isn't left to stand for hours and it's a riot of color. It tastes wonderful and doesn't need any accompaniments.

1 cup bulgur wheat	*4 scallions*
1 red bell pepper	*1 small avocado*
1 yellow bell pepper	*1 small head of*
1 garlic clove, crushed	*radicchio*
juice of ½ lemon	*8 sprigs of flat-leaf*
1–2 tbs olive oil	*parsley*
salt and freshly	
ground black pepper	
2–3 tomatoes	

1 Preheat the broiler to high. Put the bulgur wheat into a large bowl and then cover it with 1½ cups of boiling water. Leave on one side to swell while you prepare the remaining ingredients.

2 Cut the bell peppers into quarters, place them cut-side down on a broiler pan and broil for 10 minutes or until the skins have blistered and charred in places. Remove from the broiler and cover with a damp cloth.

3 Meanwhile, put the garlic into a bowl with the lemon juice, olive oil and some salt and pepper.

4 Wash and chop the tomatoes and trim and chop the scallions. Peel, pit and chop the avocado. Wash and roughly tear the radicchio and parsley. Add all these to the garlic.

5 Peel the bell peppers, pulling off the skin with a sharp knife; discard the seeds and stalks, then cut the flesh into strips and add to the other salad ingredients in the bowl.

6 Fork through the bulgur wheat, then add this to the salad and mix gently to distribute all the ingredients well, adding some salt and pepper to taste as you do so.

SERVES 2 AS A MAIN COURSE, 4–6 AS A SIDE DISH

VEGETABLE COUSCOUS

This is a quick way with couscous that may not result in every grain being immaculately separate, but who cares? It tastes good, and it doesn't need any accompaniment except perhaps a glass of spicy wine.

1 fennel bulb	8 ounces tomatoes
8 ounces carrots	8 ounces zucchini
2 tbs olive oil	1¼ cups couscous
1 onion, peeled and chopped	1 tbs butter
	1–2 tbs chopped fresh parsley
1 tbs coriander seeds	
1 garlic clove, crushed	

1 Trim off any green leafy bits from the fennel, then pare away any tough outer layers using a vegetable parer or sharp knife. Slice the fennel; scrape and slice the carrots.

2 Heat the oil in a large pan and put in the fennel, carrots and onion. Cover and leave to cook gently, with a lid on the pan, for 10 minutes.

3 Meanwhile, crush the coriander seeds in a pestle and mortar or with a wooden spoon. Then add these to the vegetables, along with the garlic.

4 Put the tomatoes into a bowl, cover with boiling water and leave for a few seconds until the skins split. Drain, cover with cold water and slip off the skins with a sharp knife. De-seed and chop the tomatoes and add them to the pan.

5 Wash, trim and slice the zucchini and add these to the pan, too. If the vegetables show any signs of sticking, add 1–2 tablespoons of water. Cover and cook for 5 minutes or until the zucchini are tender.

6 Meanwhile, prepare the couscous. Put 1¼ cups of water into a saucepan and bring to the boil. Sprinkle in the couscous, then remove the pan from the heat and leave for 2 minutes. Add the butter and a little seasoning, put the pan back on the stove and heat gently, stirring with a fork, for 3 minutes.

7 By this time the vegetables should all be tender. Check the seasoning, sprinkle with the parsley and serve with the couscous.

SERVES 2–3

SWEET COUSCOUS WITH APRICOTS

This is a very adaptable dish. While I really created it as a dessert it also makes a delicious brunch recipe, and can even be served as a salad if you put it on a base of lettuce. If you try it, you'll see what I mean. Some thick strained yogurt goes particularly well with it, however you serve it.

⅔ cup unsweetened shredded coconut	½ tsp cinnamon
	1 tbs clear honey
⅓ cup ready-to-eat dried apricots	⅔ cup couscous
	¼ cup slivered almonds
⅓ cup raisins	

1 Put the coconut in a bowl, pour over 1¼ cups of water and leave to steep for 5 minutes. Meanwhile, chop the apricots roughly, then put them into a saucepan with the raisins and enough water just to cover. Bring to the boil then cover and let simmer gently while you prepare the couscous.

2 Strain the coconut, pressing out as much liquid as possible, then put the liquid in a pan with the cinnamon and honey. Bring to the boil, then pour in the couscous. Cover and remove from the heat.

3 Heat the broiler. Spread the almonds out on a broiler pan and broil for 1–2 minutes, until they are golden brown.

4 Stir the couscous gently with a fork to separate the grains. Drain the apricots and raisins, or boil rapidly to evaporate the water, if you prefer. Add the apricots and raisins to the couscous, along with the toasted slivered almonds.

SERVES 2–4

POLENTA WITH BROILED VEGETABLES

1 tsp salt
¾ cup quick-cooking
  polenta
1 large red onion
1 large fennel bulb
2 beefsteak tomatoes

8 ounces large flat
  mushrooms
olive oil
1 or 2 sprigs of
  rosemary

1 Put 1¼ cups of water and the salt into a medium non-stick saucepan and bring to the boil, then sprinkle the polenta in and stir until smooth. Let the mixture cook gently for 4–5 minutes, until it has thickened, then tip it on to a large flat plate and quickly spread it out so that it is about ½ inch thick. Leave to cool while you prepare the vegetables. Set the broiler to high.

2 Bring 2 inches of water to the boil in another pan for the onion and fennel. Peel the onion. Trim the fennel by removing any tough leaves or pieces of stalk but leaving enough stalk to hold the leaves together at the base. Cut the fennel and the onion down first into halves, then into quarters and eighths.

3 Cook the onion and fennel in the boiling water for about 6–8 minutes or until they are just tender without being at all soggy. Drain well and dry on paper towels.

4 Thickly slice the tomatoes; wash and trim the mushrooms.

5 Brush all the vegetables with olive oil, then arrange them on a broiler pan, sprinkle with the leaves from the rosemary sprigs and broil for about 15 minutes or until lightly charred on both sides, turning as necessary.

6 Meanwhile, cut the polenta into triangles and fry them in olive oil in a skillet for about 4–5 minutes per side, until crisp and lightly browned. Drain the polenta on paper towels and serve with the vegetables.

SERVES 2

OPPOSITE: *Polenta with Broiled Vegetables*

VARIATION

POLENTA WITH GARLIC MAYONNAISE AND SALAD

Make the polenta as described above. Serve the fried polenta with a lettuce, tomato and scallion salad and some garlic mayonnaise made by stirring 1 crushed garlic clove into 4 tablespoons of mayonnaise, or a mixture of mayonnaise and yogurt.

OLIVE POLENTA WITH TOMATO SAUCE

1 tsp salt
¾ cup quick-cooking
  polenta
⅓ cup olives, green or
  black or a mixture
olive oil
1 onion, peeled and
  chopped

1 garlic clove, crushed
1¾ cups canned
  tomatoes
salt and freshly
  ground black pepper

1 Put 1¼ cups of water and the salt into a medium non-stick saucepan and bring to the boil, then sprinkle the polenta in and stir until smooth. Cook gently for 4–5 minutes, until it has thickened.

2 Pit the olives and stir them into the cooked polenta, then tip it on to a large flat plate and quickly spread it out so that it is about ½ inch thick. Leave to cool while you prepare the sauce.

3 Heat 1 tablespoon of oil in a pan then add the onion, cover and cook gently for 10 minutes. Add the garlic and cook for 1–2 minutes, then stir in the tomatoes together with their juice, breaking them up with a wooden spoon. Simmer for 10–15 minutes until the excess liquid has evaporated.

4 Meanwhile, cut the polenta into pieces and fry in olive oil for about 4–5 minutes per side until crisp and lightly browned. Drain on paper towels.

5 Season the sauce with salt and pepper and serve with the polenta.

SERVES 2

I have recently discovered quick-cooking polenta, which I find excellent – it brings polenta into the fast-food category and I prefer the flavor to that of traditional slow-cooking polenta. Serve it with broiled vegetables for a meal that really brings the Mediterranean sunshine with it.

The olives give this a pleasant salty tang. Serve with a refreshing side salad.

NUTS
— * —

LITTLE NUT CROQUETTES WITH CAPER SAUCE

Serve these crunchy nut croquettes with a quick-cooking vegetable such as snow peas or green beans, or with a crisp green salad or a tomato, avocado and basil salad. Some mashed potatoes go well with them, too, for a more substantial meal.

4 tbs butter
4 tbs flour
1 bay leaf
2½ cups milk
1 large onion, peeled and finely chopped
1 tbs olive oil
4 slices of bread
1 cup cashews
1 cup pecans
salt and freshly ground black pepper
3 tbs capers
2 tsp wine vinegar
2 tbs snipped fresh chives
oil for deep-frying

1 Melt the butter in a medium saucepan and stir in the flour. Cook for 1–2 minutes, stirring, then add the bay leaf and half the milk; bring to a simmer and stir until very thick. Put half the mixture in a bowl and set aside. Then stir the remaining milk into the pan, beating hard until smooth. Let the sauce simmer very gently for a few minutes.

2 Meanwhile, gently fry the onion in the oil for 5–10 minutes, until lightly browned.

3 Break the bread into chunks and put it into a food processor with the cashews and pecans; whizz until they are all finely chopped.

4 Add the reserved thick sauce to the onion, along with the nuts and breadcrumbs and some salt and pepper to taste. Add a little water, if necessary, for a firm but soft and pliable consistency. Form the mixture into 20 balls roughly the size of walnuts.

5 Add the capers, vinegar, chives and some salt and pepper to the sauce, then keep warm.

6 Heat some oil for deep-frying in a saucepan, wok or deep-fat fryer. Test the temperature by dipping a wooden chopstick or the handle of a wooden spoon into it: the oil should immediately form bubbles around it. Put in the croquettes and fry for 4–5 minutes, until brown and crisp. Drain on paper towels and serve at once, in a pool of the sauce.
SERVES 4

CHESTNUT AND MUSHROOM CASSEROLE

This goes well with mashed potatoes or, better still, baked potatoes – the timing of these will fit in if you allow the longer cooking time for the casserole.

5 outer stalks from 1 head of celery
2 large carrots
2 large leeks
2 tbs olive oil
1 large onion, peeled and chopped
2 cups fresh mushrooms
2 garlic cloves, crushed
9 ounces canned whole chestnuts
2 tbs plain flour
large sprig of thyme
⅔ cup red wine
2 tbs soy sauce
salt and freshly ground black pepper
chopped fresh parsley

1 Wash, trim and slice the celery. Put it into a saucepan with 2½ cups of water and bring to the boil. Scrape and slice the carrots; wash, trim and slice the leeks. Add all these to the pan.

2 While the vegetables simmer away, heat the oil in another pan and fry the onion for 5 minutes. Slice the mushrooms and add to the onion, along with the garlic. Stir and cook for 5 minutes.

3 Add the chestnuts to the onion mixture, then stir in the flour and cook for 2 minutes. Tip in the vegetables from the other pan, with their water.

4 Add the thyme, wine, soy sauce and seasoning and then simmer gently until all the vegetables are tender. This may take only 10 minutes, but if you have time to cook it for longer – up to 45 minutes – the flavors will improve. Serve sprinkled with chopped parsley.
SERVES 4

OPPOSITE: *(top) Chestnut and Mushroom Casserole and (bottom) Little Nut Croquettes with Caper Sauce*

CHESTNUTS WITH SAVOY CABBAGE AND SAGE

This is a particularly warming and delicious dish for the fall and winter. Do use Savoy cabbage if you can get it because its flavor is the best, although other types of cabbage can be used as well. I like this as a main course, served with some light, creamy mashed potatoes.

2 tbs butter
1 onion, peeled and
  sliced
1 garlic clove, crushed
½ Savoy cabbage,
  about 4 cups, packed,
  after shredding

9 ounces canned whole
  chestnuts
2–3 sprigs of sage
salt and freshly
  ground black pepper

1 Melt the butter in a medium saucepan and put in the onion; stir, then cover and cook gently for 5 minutes. Add the garlic, then cover and cook for 1–2 minutes longer.

2 Meanwhile, wash and coarsely shred the cabbage, then cook it in ½ inch of boiling water for about 7 minutes or until just tender.

3 Add the chestnuts to the onion mixture in the pan, mashing them a bit to break them up. Heat gently until the chestnuts are warmed through.

4 Drain the cabbage thoroughly and add it to the chestnut mixture. Tear in the sage leaves, then season everything well with salt and pepper and serve immediately.

SERVES 2

NUT PATE WITH DATE AND MINT CHUTNEY

This is one of the nicest nut pâté mixtures I know. It's equally good hot or cold, with a cooked vegetable such as green beans or a salad. The chutney makes a delicious accompaniment, but if you don't have time to prepare it the pâté is equally good without it.

⅔ cup low-fat garlic-
  and herb-flavored
  cream cheese, such as
  Boursin
1¼ cups roasted cashews
dash of Tabasco or
  hot pepper sauce
  (optional)
1 cup dry
  breadcrumbs
  (optional)

FOR THE CHUTNEY
4 ounces dates
1 small onion, peeled
  and chopped
1 tbs wine vinegar
2 tbs chopped fresh
  mint
pinch of cayenne
  pepper
salt and freshly
  ground black pepper

1 Make the chutney first to allow time for the flavors to develop: chop the dates then put them into a saucepan with the onion, vinegar and 3 tablespoons of water. Cover and cook gently for about 5 minutes, until both have softened and the mixture is no longer liquid.

2 Remove from the heat and add the chopped mint, cayenne pepper and some salt and pepper to taste. Transfer to a bowl and leave on one side.

3 Next make the pâté: put the cheese into a bowl and mash until soft and creamy. Grind the nuts in a food processor or with a rotary hand grater.

4 Stir the nuts into the cheese to form a mixture that is soft but will hold its shape. Add the Tabasco, if you wish, and season with salt and pepper.

5 Form the pâté into a log shape, then coat it all over with the breadcrumbs, if you are using these.

6 Serve the pâté as it is (it can be chilled until needed, in which case it will firm up a bit more), or put it under a moderately hot broiler and broil for about 3 minutes each on the top, bottom and sides, until crisp and brown and heated right through. Cut into 6 slices and serve with the date and mint chutney, if you're having this.

SERVES 2

Different types of nuts can be used in the pâté, but they are best if they are roasted first. This can be done under the grill or in the oven at 350°F (180°C) for about 20 minutes, until golden brown. In the case of hazelnuts, rub off the skins, in a soft cloth. For speed, use ready-roasted nuts.

CELERY ALMONDINE

This simple dish consists of celery in a creamy sauce with a base and topping of slivered almonds. Serve as an appetizer or a side dish, or with some boiled new potatoes for a light and unusual main course.

1 head of celery or 2 celery hearts	**1 cup slivered almonds**
1 bay leaf	**a little milk (optional)**
2 tbs butter	**2 tbs flour**
1 onion, peeled and chopped	**2 tbs cream**
	salt and freshly ground black pepper

1 Wash and trim the celery, removing any damaged or tough stalks, then chop it quite finely: do this by cutting down the length of each stalk several times to produce long, thin strips then cutting across to produce little dice.

2 Put the celery into a saucepan with the bay leaf and water just to cover, then bring to the boil, cover and simmer for about 15 minutes or until the celery is very tender.

3 Meanwhile, melt the butter in a saucepan, add the onion and cook gently, covered, for about 5 minutes or until softened.

4 Heat the broiler. Spread half the almonds out on a broiler pan and broil for 1–2 minutes, until golden brown. Remove from the broiler, leaving the broiler on.

5 Drain the celery, reserving the liquid and making it up to 1¼ cups if necessary with some water or a little milk.

6 Stir the flour into the onion and cook for 1–2 minutes. Then add the celery liquid, stirring all the time. Simmer gently over a very low heat for about 5 minutes. Add the celery and continue to cook gently until the celery is heated through.

7 Scatter the toasted almonds evenly over the base of a shallow gratin dish. Stir the cream into the celery mixture, season with salt and pepper, then spoon it into the dish on top of the almonds. Sprinkle the remaining, untoasted, almonds on top and put it under the broiler until the almonds are golden brown and everything is piping hot.

SERVES 2 AS A MAIN COURSE

CHESTNUT FOOL

9 ounces canned unsweetened chestnut purée	**2 tbs brandy or Armagnac**
½ cup confectioners' sugar	**1¼ cups heavy cream**
	candied chestnuts and/or grated chocolate to decorate

1 Put the chestnut purée into a large bowl with the confectioners' sugar and brandy or Armagnac and beat it until it is smooth.

2 Whisk the cream until it is thick but not standing in peaks, then fold it into the chestnut mixture.

3 Spoon the mixture into small glasses and decorate with candied chestnuts or grated chocolate (or both). Chill until needed.

SERVES 6

ALMOND AND CHOCOLATE SLICES

7 ounces good-quality milk chocolate	**⅔ cup raisins**
	1½ cups cornflakes
1 cup slivered almonds	

1 Break the chocolate into pieces and put it into a large bowl set over a pan of steaming water. Leave until the chocolate has melted. Meanwhile, line an 8-inch square cake pan with parchment paper.

2 Remove the bowl of chocolate from the pan. Add the slivered almonds and raisins then add the cornflakes, crushing them with your hands as you do so; they need to be slightly powdery.

3 Mix thoroughly, then spoon the mixture into the pan, spreading it right into the corners and pressing it down well. Put the pan in the fridge or even the freezer if you are very rushed. It will set in about 10–15 minutes and can then be turned out, stripped of the paper, and cut into pieces.

MAKES 9

This dessert can be whizzed up at a moment's notice. Stand the can of chestnut purée on a radiator or in a pan of very hot water for a few minutes before using it, if there's time, because then it will be soft and easy to mix.

This is a variation on the well-known cornflakes-and-chocolate crunchies adored by children. It's a useful recipe if you need to produce home-made cookies in a hurry.

VEGETABLES

Vegetables are excellent fast foods and make the basis of hundreds of speedy dishes. Most are quick to cook or can be served raw, and now that you can buy many of them ready washed the preparation time is even quicker. They can be made into wonderful main courses such as Provençal Potatoes, Broccoli with Cashew Sauce or Broiled Mediterranean Vegetables with Mozzarella; comforting soups, including Green Pea and Mint and Creamy Onion; or salads such as Thai Cabbage Salad or Italian Country Salad; vegetables are so versatile that there's plenty of scope for experiment.

SOUPS & TOP-OF-THE-STOVE DISHES

✳

GREEN PEA AND MINT SOUP

If you're looking for a quick soup this one is hard to beat. Although it can be made all year round, it has a refreshing summery flavor.

1 tbs butter	**salt and freshly ground**
1 onion, peeled and	**black pepper**
chopped	**1–2 tbs lemon juice**
1 small potato, diced	
1 pound frozen peas	
4–5 sprigs of mint	

1 Melt the butter in a large saucepan and gently fry the onion and potato for about 10 minutes.

2 Add the peas, the leaves from the mint sprigs, and 4 cups of water. Bring to the boil, then simmer gently for 10–15 minutes or until the potato and onion are tender.

3 Purée the soup in a blender, then pour it through a strainer back into the pan. Thin with a little water if you like, then reheat. Season well with salt and pepper and a good squeeze of lemon juice.
SERVES 4

QUICK VEGETABLE SOUP

Although this soup is very quick to make, the vegetables are cooked slowly in oil initially, which really helps them to release their flavor.

8 ounces carrots	**2 tbs chopped fresh**
8 ounces parsnips	**parsley**
8 ounces leeks	**salt and freshly**
1 tbs light olive oil	**ground black pepper**
1¾ cups canned	
tomatoes	

1 Scrape the carrots and cut them into tiny dice. Peel the parsnips and dice them in the same way then trim the leeks and slice them finely.

2 Heat the oil in a large saucepan and put in the vegetables. Cover and cook gently for 10 minutes, then add the tomatoes with their juice and 2½ cups of water. Bring to the boil then reduce the heat and simmer for about 15 minutes, until tender.

3 Add the parsley, season with salt and pepper, then serve in warmed bowls.
SERVES 2–3

CREAMY ONION SOUP

1½ pounds	**3–4 tbs light cream**
potatoes	**(optional)**
1½ pounds onions	**salt and freshly**
2 tbs butter	**ground black pepper**
	freshly grated nutmeg

1 Peel and dice the potatoes and put them into a saucepan with 2 cups of water. Bring to the boil, then cover and simmer for 15–20 minutes, until very tender. Meanwhile, peel the onions and slice them into half-circles.

2 Melt the butter in another saucepan and put in the onions. Cover and cook over a gentle heat until tender. This will take about 15 minutes and they'll need stirring from time to time to prevent sticking.

3 When the potatoes are done, either mash them very thoroughly in their water or, which is easier, whizz them to a purée in a food processor then return them to the pan.

4 Tip the onions and their liquid into the potato purée and add the cream, if you're using this. Thin the soup with a little more water, reheat gently, then season with salt, pepper and freshly grated nutmeg.
SERVES 4

This is a very adaptable vegetable soup: throw in a handful of small pasta and add a little extra liquid 10 minutes before serving to make it more substantial: and/or add a can of navy or cannellini beans. For a Mediterranean flavor, stir in a couple of spoonfuls of pesto just before you serve it. Eat it as it is, or with grated cheese on top. Some country-style bread goes well with it, too.

ROOT VEGETABLES STEWED IN OIL AND BUTTER

A warming dish for winter and one of my favorite ways of cooking root vegetables. You can use any combination you like: celery root, Jerusalem artichokes, turnips and kohlrabi are all good. Serve as a main course, with some coarse country-style bread.

8 ounces onions	2 tbs butter
8 ounces carrots	salt and freshly
8 ounces parsnips	ground black pepper
8 ounces sweet	a little chopped fresh
potatoes	parsley, if available
2 tbs olive oil	

1 Peel and chop the onions; scrape the carrots and slice them thinly. Peel and slice the parsnips and sweet potatoes – these can be in slightly bigger pieces.

2 Heat the oil and butter in a large saucepan and put in the vegetables. Cook very gently, with a lid on the pan, for 15–20 minutes or until tender.

3 Season with salt and pepper and scatter with a little chopped parsley, if available.

SERVES 2

VARIATION

LEEKS AND POTATOES STEWED IN OIL AND BUTTER

Substitute 1 pound of potatoes and 1 pound of leeks for the root vegetables. Peel the potatoes and cut them into quite chunky slices; wash the leeks and slice them fairly thickly. Then proceed as above.

BROCCOLI WITH CASHEW SAUCE

Creamy and lightly spiced, this is delicious served with plain rice and some Indian bread.

1 tbs oil	½ tsp turmeric
1 onion, peeled and	1 cup cashews
chopped	salt and freshly
1 cinnamon stick,	ground black pepper
broken	1–2 tbs lemon juice
small piece of fresh	(optional)
ginger root	1 pound broccoli
1 garlic clove, crushed	
6–8 cardamom pods	

1 Heat the oil in a medium saucepan, add the onion and the cinnamon stick then cover and cook gently for 5 minutes, until the onion has softened. Grate the ginger on the fine side of a grater, add the ginger and the garlic to the onion, cover again and cook for 2–3 minutes.

2 Crush the cardamom so that the seeds come out of the pods; discard the pods and crush the seeds a bit. Stir these into the onion along with the turmeric and cook for 1–2 minutes longer.

3 Take the cinnamon out of the pan but don't throw it away. Tip the onion mixture into a food processor and add the cashews and 1¼ cups of water. Whizz thoroughly until creamy.

4 Tip the mixture back into the pan and add the cinnamon stick again. Season with salt and pepper, sharpen with a little lemon juice if necessary, then reheat the sauce gently and keep it warm while you prepare the broccoli.

5 Wash the broccoli and divide it into flowerets. Peel the stalks thickly to remove any tough skin, then slice them into rounds or matchsticks. Cook the broccoli in 1 inch of boiling water for about 3–4 minutes, until tender; don't let it get soggy. Drain immediately and season lightly.

6 You can mix the broccoli into the cashew sauce or pour a little of the sauce on to warmed serving plates, top with the broccoli and pour the remaining sauce on top – this looks more attractive.

SERVES 2

Many other vegetables can be substituted for the broccoli: try carrots, green beans, cauliflower, pumpkin, okra, or a mixture.

LEMONY SPRING VEGETABLES

Colcannon consists of cooked cabbage or kale, onion or leeks and creamy mashed potatoes, mixed together and served with a pool of melted butter. It is an old Irish dish, traditionally eaten at Hallowe'en, but it's quick to make, cheap, soothing and delicious any time.

*8 ounces tiny new
  potatoes
8 ounces baby carrots
8 ounces baby turnips
  or fennel
8 ounces young green
  beans, or fava beans
  still in their pods*

*1–2 tbs butter
chopped fresh herbs,
  such as mint, parsley,
  chives, tarragon or
  chervil
squeeze of lemon juice
salt and freshly
  ground black pepper*

1 Bring 2 inches of water to the boil in a large pan. Meanwhile, clean and trim the vegetables as necessary.

2 Put the vegetables into the boiling water, adding them according to the time they will take to cook: about 10 minutes for the potatoes and carrots; 6–8 minutes for the turnips and fennel; and 2 minutes for the beans. Cook until just tender.

3 Drain the vegetables, add the butter, herbs, lemon juice and seasoning, then serve at once.
SERVES 2

PROVENCAL POTATOES

This is good served with green salad or some baby spinach – for speed, buy spinach ready washed and microwave it in the packet, or cook it without water in a pan for a few minutes until just wilted.

*1 onion, peeled and
  chopped
1 tbs olive oil
1 garlic clove, crushed
1¾ cups canned
  tomatoes
12 ounces potatoes
2 sun-dried tomatoes
  in oil, drained*

*⅓ cup Kalamata olives
salt and freshly
  ground black pepper
shavings of fresh
  Parmesan cheese
  (optional)*

1 Fry the onion in the oil for 5 minutes, then add the garlic and the canned tomatoes, breaking the tomatoes up with a wooden spoon. Bring to the boil and simmer for 10–15 minutes, until very thick.

2 Meanwhile, bring 2 inches of water to the boil for the potatoes. Peel the potatoes then cut them into slices ¼ inch thick. Add to the pan, cover and simmer for 7–10 minutes, until tender but not breaking up, then drain.

3 Chop the sun-dried tomatoes and add to the sauce along with half the olives. Season, then mix together the sauce and the potatoes, top with the remaining olives and serve immediately. Or top with Parmesan cheese, brown under the broiler, then garnish with the remaining olives and serve.
SERVES 2

COLCANNON

*1½ pounds potatoes
1½ pounds kale or
  dark cabbage
2 leeks*

*½ cup milk or light
  cream
4 tbs butter
salt and freshly
  ground black pepper*

1 Peel and dice the potatoes then boil for 15–20 minutes, until tender.

2 Meanwhile, wash the kale or cabbage, remove any tough stalks and shred the rest coarsely. Cook, covered, in ½ inch of boiling water for 15–20 minutes: it needs cooking for longer than usual.

3 Clean and trim the leeks then slice them quite finely. Put them into a saucepan with the milk or cream and simmer gently for 5–6 minutes, until tender. Put the butter into a small bowl and set it on top of the pan of leeks to melt the butter.

4 Drain the kale or cabbage and quickly chop it. Put it back in the pan to keep warm.

5 Drain the potatoes and mash with the leeks and milk or cream. Mix in the kale and season well. Transfer the mixture to heated plates, make a well in the center and pour the melted butter into it.
SERVES 4

OPPOSITE: *(left) Quick Vegetable Soup, page 98,
(right) Lemony Spring Vegetables,
(bottom) Provençal Potatoes*

GRATINS & BROILED VEGETABLES

✳

CHEESY VEGETABLE GRATIN

This works best if you use a big shallow gratin dish so that you end up with quite a thin layer of vegetables and lots of lovely, golden cheesy topping. You can use a variety of different vegetables; choose ones that take about the same time to cook, or add them to the boiling water in succession, according to their cooking time.

8 ounces carrots	**salt and freshly**
8 ounces fennel	**ground black pepper**
8 ounces zucchini	
4–6 ounces Gruyère	
or Cheddar	
cheese	

1 Scrape the carrots and slice them thinly, then put them into a saucepan, pour over boiling water to cover, and simmer for 5 minutes while you prepare the fennel.

2 Trim the fennel, paring away any tough parts on the outer leaves, then slice it into slightly bigger pieces than the carrots. Add to the pan and cook for 5 more minutes.

3 Meanwhile, wash and trim the zucchini, then slice them thinly and add to the pan. Cook for 2–3 minutes, until all the vegetables are tender.

4 Heat the broiler. Drain the vegetables (keep the water, if you like; it makes excellent soup stock). Put the vegetables into a shallow gratin dish and season them lightly. Then grate or slice the cheese, arrange it on top of the vegetables and put the dish under the broiler for 7–10 minutes, until the cheese is golden brown and bubbling.

SERVES 2

Balsamic vinegar has a wonderful sweet, mellow flavor and comes in a wide price range, depending on how long it has been aged. A few drops of even a modestly priced one (which is what I use most of the time) will do wonders for many foods.

BROILED FENNEL PLATTER

Tender, slightly sweet broiled fennel is combined here with peppery leaves, tangy red bell peppers and creamy hummus or soft cheese. Serve this platter with some good warm bread.

2 red bell peppers	**1 cup arugula or**
2 large fennel bulbs	**watercress**
1 tbs olive oil	**½ cup hummus or soft**
dash of balsamic	**cheese, such as white**
vinegar	**goat cheese, farmer's**
salt and freshly	**cheese or ricotta**
ground black pepper	

1 Heat the broiler. Cut the bell peppers into quarters, place them cut-side down on a broiler pan and broil on high for 10–15 minutes, until the skins have blistered and charred in places. Remove from the broiler and cover with a damp cloth.

2 Meanwhile, bring 1 inch of water to the boil in a saucepan. Trim the fennel, paring away any tough parts on the outer leaves and cutting off the feathery top, then cut it into either six or eight pieces that still hold together at the base. Add to the boiling water, cook for about 8 minutes, until almost completely tender, then drain (keep the water, if you like; it makes excellent soup stock).

3 Toss the fennel in the oil so that the pieces are completely coated, then spread them out on a broiler pan and broil under a high heat for 5–10 minutes or until they are lightly browned, turning them halfway through.

4 Meanwhile, peel and de-seed the red peppers and cut them into strips.

5 Season the fennel and peppers with the balsamic vinegar and salt and pepper to taste. Mix them together if you like, and arrange them on a platter with the arugula or watercress and the hummus or soft cheese.

SERVES 2

BUTTERNUT SQUASH AND GOAT CHEESE GRATIN

This unusual gratin is excellent served with a Belgian endive and walnut salad.

1 butternut squash, about 2½ pounds
1 tbs butter
1 onion, peeled and chopped
1 garlic clove, crushed
salt and freshly ground black pepper
7 ounces firm goat cheese

1 Peel and de-seed the butternut squash, then cut the flesh into long slices about ¼ inch thick. Put them into a saucepan and pour over boiling water to cover, then simmer for about 7 minutes, until the squash is tender.

2 Meanwhile, melt the butter in a saucepan, add the onion and garlic, cover and cook gently for about 5 minutes, until the onion is tender.

3 Heat the broiler. Drain the butternut squash, reserving the liquid, then return the squash to the pan and add the onion and garlic. You can mash the butternut squash, adding a little of the reserved liquid, if you wish, or leave it as it is. In any case, season with salt and pepper.

4 Put the mixture into a shallow gratin dish. Then slice the cheese thinly, including the rind, and arrange it on top in overlapping slices, like roof tiles. Put it under the broiler for 7–10 minutes, until the cheese is golden brown.

SERVES 4

CAULIFLOWER TOMATO CHEESE

This tasty and colorful variation of an old favorite is good served with a crisp green salad, a quickly cooked green vegetable or something easy such as frozen peas or green beans.

1 tbs olive oil
1 onion, peeled and chopped
1 garlic clove, crushed
1¾ cups canned tomatoes
1 small to medium cauliflower
salt and freshly ground black pepper
1 cup grated Cheddar or Gruyère cheese

1 First make the tomato sauce: heat the olive oil in a medium pan then fry the onion in it for 5 minutes, until beginning to soften. Add the garlic and tomatoes, breaking the tomatoes up roughly with a wooden spoon.

2 Bring to the boil and let the mixture simmer away for 10–15 minutes, until it is very thick and any excess liquid has evaporated.

3 Meanwhile, wash and trim the cauliflower, breaking it up into even-sized florets. Cook it in 2 inches of boiling water for about 5 minutes, until tender, then drain.

4 Heat the broiler. Mix the cauliflower florets with the tomato sauce and season well with salt and pepper. Spoon it into a shallow gratin dish, sprinkle with the grated cheese and broil until the cheese is golden brown.

SERVES 2–3

Various types of cheese can be used for this: try blue cheese or feta for a tangy flavor.

MUSHROOMS STUFFED WITH FETA AND RED ONION

These are good served on a base of shredded crisp lettuce, though you could serve them on rounds of toast or fried bread, if you prefer.

1 red onion	**6 large flat mushrooms**
olive oil	**4 ounces feta cheese**

[1] Peel the onion then slice it into thin rings. Heat 1 tablespoon of oil in a pan, add the onion, cover and cook gently for 5–10 minutes, until tender.

[2] Heat the broiler to high. Wipe the mushrooms and remove the stalks. Brush the caps lightly with olive oil, then place them on a broiler pan and broil for 5–10 minutes, until tender and lightly browned. To check if they are done, turn them over and look underneath – it should be moist and tender.

[3] Cut the feta cheese into ¼-inch cubes. Mix these with the onion in the pan (off the heat).

[4] Turn all the mushrooms so that the gills are uppermost, then divide the cheese mixture between them. Put them back under the broiler for 5–10 minutes, until the cheese has melted and browned and the mushrooms are piping hot. Serve at once.
SERVES 2

BROILED MEDITERRANEAN VEGETABLES WITH MOZZARELLA

1 large eggplant, about 12 ounces	**12 ounces tomatoes, preferably cherry tomatoes**
12 ounces zucchini	**8 ounces Mozzarella cheese**
2 tbs olive oil	**sprigs of basil**
salt and freshly ground black pepper	

This only needs some good bread – perhaps an Italian-style loaf – to accompany it.

[1] Set the broiler to high. Cut the eggplant into pieces about ¼ inch thick, 2 inches long and 1 inch wide; slice the zucchini into ¼-inch rounds. Put them on a broiler pan, then sprinkle with the olive oil and some salt and pepper and, using your hands, mix the vegetables so that they all get coated with oil.

[2] Put the vegetables under the broiler for about 10 minutes, turning them as necessary. Then add the tomatoes – cherry tomatoes whole, others quartered – and broil for a further 5 minutes.

[3] Meanwhile, cut the Mozzarella cheese into smallish chunks and add these to the vegetables. Broil for about 5 minutes longer, until the cheese has melted and browned lightly, then tear the basil over the top and serve at once.
SERVES 2

PARSNIP AND HAZELNUT GRATIN

This goes well with some peppery watercress for a quick light lunch or evening meal.

1½ pounds parsnips	**salt and freshly ground black pepper**
1 tbs butter	**1 cup hazelnuts**
⅔ cup sour cream	

[1] Peel the parsnips and cut them into even-sized pieces. Put them in a saucepan, pour over boiling water to cover and simmer for about 10 minutes, until tender.

[2] Heat the broiler. Drain the parsnips, add the butter and mash well, then stir in the sour cream and season with salt and pepper to taste.

[3] Spoon the mixture into a shallow gratin dish. Crush the hazelnuts with a rolling pin or whizz them briefly in a food processor. Scatter them on top of the parsnip mixture.

[4] Put the dish under the broiler for 5 minutes or so, until the hazelnuts are golden brown.
SERVES 2

OPPOSITE: *Broiled Mediterranean Vegetables with Mozzarella*

POTATO WEDGES

———— ✳ ————

Baked potatoes are a wonderful convenience food because they are so quick to prepare, but the drawback is the long cooking time. Here is a version that is both fast to prepare and fast to cook. This is achieved by cutting and parboiling the potatoes first, then brushing them with olive oil and broiling them to cook them through. They're best served with moist toppings and dips, and a simple crisp salad such as Bibb lettuce or Belgian endive and watercress.

BASIC RECIPE

2 potatoes,   olive oil
    8–12 ounces each   sea salt

1 Scrub the potatoes, cut each one in half lengthways and then in half again, to make four long wedges.

2 Put the potato wedges into a saucepan, pour over boiling water to cover and bring back to the boil. Cook for 5 minutes from the time the water boils, then drain thoroughly.

3 Meanwhile, heat the broiler. Brush the drained potato wedges all over with olive oil, then put them on a cookie sheet or a broiler pan and place them under the broiler.

4 Broil on high for 10–15 minutes, until the potatoes are tender right through and golden brown, turning them as necessary. Remove from the broiler, sprinkle with sea salt, then serve with any of the toppings below.
SERVES 2

VARIATIONS

1 POTATO WEDGES WITH HERBS

Sprinkle the potatoes with fresh rosemary or thyme before broiling; caraway seeds are good, too, if you like the flavor.

2 POTATO STEAKS

These are made in the same way, except that this time you cut the potatoes into slices about ½ inch thick – like steaks – instead of into wedges.

TOPPINGS

All these toppings make enough for two large potatoes. As well as the recipes below, you could try the following suggestions: sour cream mixed with horseradish cream or snipped fresh chives; guacamole (see page 21); good-quality store-bought pesto or homemade (see page 59); soft goat cheese, cream cheese or cottage cheese; hummus; garlic butter; or, of course, plenty of butter and grated cheese.

— 1 —

MUSHROOMS IN SOUR CREAM

8 ounces Cremini   salt and freshly
    (brown cap)   ground black pepper
    mushrooms   snipped fresh chives
2 tbs butter
1 garlic clove, crushed
⅔ cup sour cream

1 Wipe and slice the mushrooms. Melt the butter in a saucepan and add the mushrooms then cook, uncovered, for about 5 minutes, until tender.

2 Add the garlic and cook for a further 1–2 minutes, then remove from the heat.

3 Just before you are ready to serve, put the pan back on the heat and get the mushrooms sizzling again. Then add the sour cream and stir until it has heated through; don't let it boil or it will curdle. Remove from the heat, season, and serve with some snipped chives on top.

— 2 —
RED AND YELLOW PEPPER SALSA

Start making this before you prepare the potato wedges, so the peppers can be broiling while you scrub and boil the potatoes.

1 red bell pepper	**salt and freshly**
1 yellow bell pepper	**ground black pepper**
2 large tomatoes	

1   Heat the broiler. Cut the peppers in half and put them cut-side down on a broiler pan, then broil them under a fierce heat until they are blistered and charred in places. Remove them from the broiler and cover with a damp dish towel.

2   Pour boiling water over the tomatoes, leave for a few seconds until the skins loosen, then drain them and cover with cold water. Remove the skins with a sharp knife. Chop the tomatoes and put them into a bowl.

3   Remove the skin from the bell pepper halves – it will peel off easily – and also remove any seeds. Thinly slice the peppers and add to the tomatoes. Mix well and season with salt and pepper.

— 3 —
CHILI-TOMATO SAUCE

1 tbs olive oil	**chili powder**
1 onion, peeled and	**salt, freshly ground**
chopped	**black pepper and**
1 garlic clove, crushed	**sugar**
1¾ cups canned	
tomatoes	

1   Heat the oil in a saucepan, then put in the onion, cover and cook for 10 minutes.

2   Stir in the garlic and cook for 1–2 minutes, then pour in the tomatoes, breaking them up with the spoon. Add a pinch or so of chili powder to taste. Cook for 10–15 minutes, uncovered, until the mixture is thick.

3   Season with salt and pepper then add extra chili powder if the sauce needs more of a kick, and a pinch of sugar if necessary.

— 4 —
BOURSIN CHEESE

Put a packet of garlic- and herb-flavored Boursin cheese into a bowl and add 2 tablespoons of hot water. Beat it until it is smooth and creamy, adding more water if necessary to achieve this consistency.

— 5 —
ROMESCO SAUCE

1 red bell pepper	**piece of dried red chili**
olive oil	**or a pinch of chili**
1 slice of white bread	**powder**
¼ cup slivered	**1 tomato, peeled and**
almonds	**quartered**
1 small garlic clove,	**salt and freshly**
peeled	**ground black pepper**
	balsamic vinegar

1   Heat the broiler. Cut the bell pepper in half, put the halves cut-side down on a broiler pan and broil under a fierce heat for about 10 minutes, until they are blistered and charred in places. Remove from the broiler and cover with a damp dish towel.

2   Meanwhile, heat a little olive oil in a skillet and fry the bread until it is crisp and golden brown on both sides. Then remove it from the skillet and put in the almonds, frying them until they are golden brown.

3   When the bell pepper is cool enough to handle, peel off the skin, remove the seeds and stalk, and cut the pepper into rough chunks. Put it into a food processor with the bread, roughly torn, and the almonds, garlic, chili and tomato. Whizz to a creamy purée.

4   Season with salt and coarsely ground black pepper then mix in a few drops of balsamic vinegar to taste.

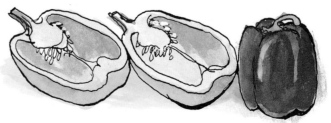

— 6 —
CREAMY CORN

2 tbs butter
2 tbs flour
1¼ cups milk
½–1 red bell pepper,
  chopped (optional)

1 cup frozen corn
  kernels
salt and freshly
  ground black pepper

[1] Melt the butter in a saucepan, then stir in the flour. Let it cook for a minute or two, then stir in the milk. Bring it to the boil, stirring, to make a smooth sauce. If you are using the red bell pepper, add this now, then leave the sauce to simmer over a low heat for 5 minutes.

[2] Add the frozen corn kernels and cook for a further 3–4 minutes, then season to taste with salt and pepper.

— 7 —
CHEDDAR CHEESE AND SCALLION DIP

1 tbs soft butter
1 cup grated Cheddar
  cheese
4 tbs light cream or
  milk

2 scallions
salt and freshly
  ground black pepper

[1] Put the butter into a bowl and add the cheese and cream or milk. Beat to make a creamy mixture.

[2] Trim and chop the scallions, then stir them into the dip and season to taste.

— 8 —
GREEN HERB MAYONNAISE

Put 4 tablespoons of good-quality mayonnaise, or 2 tablespoons of mayonnaise and 2 tablespoons of yogurt, into a small bowl and stir in 4 tablespoons of finely chopped fresh herbs, such as parsley, chives, tarragon or chervil.

OPPOSITE: *Baked Potato Wedges and Steaks topped with Pesto, Romesco Sauce and herbs*

— 9 —
VERY MINTY TZATZIKI

½ cucumber
salt and freshly
  ground black pepper
⅔ cup thick strained
  yogurt

½ garlic clove, crushed
4 tbs chopped fresh
  mint

[1] Peel the cucumber and cut it into small dice. Put these into a strainer, sprinkle with salt, cover with a plate and a weight and leave on one side to draw out excess moisture.

[2] Put the yogurt into a bowl and mix in the garlic and most of the fresh mint.

[3] Just before you are ready to serve, pat the cucumber dry on paper towels, then stir it into the yogurt mixture. Check the seasoning, then sprinkle the rest of the mint on top.

— 10 —
COLESLAW

Home-made coleslaw is so much nicer than the bought variety and it's dead simple to make.

4 ounces cabbage,
  about 2 cups, packed,
  after shredding
2 small carrots
8 tbs mayonnaise, or a
  mixture of mayon-
  naise and yogurt

2 scallions (optional)
salt and freshly
  ground black pepper

[1] Wash the cabbage, then shred it finely and put it into a bowl.

[2] Scrub or scrape the carrots then grate them into the bowl.

[3] Stir in the mayonnaise or mayonnaise and yogurt. Trim and chop the scallions, if you're using them, and add them to the bowl, too. Season with salt and pepper to taste.

SPICED VEGETABLE DISHES
✳

SPICED MIXED VEGETABLES IN CREAMY SAUCE

This is a very simple spiced vegetable dish and I think it's nicest served with some plain basmati rice. You can substitute all kinds of different vegetables for the ones listed here, and if you don't like the idea of the sour cream you could substitute light cream or even milk.

There's no need to peel fresh ginger if you're grating it: just use a fairly fine grater.

6 ounces carrots
6 ounces potatoes
6 ounces zucchini
1 cup frozen peas
2 tbs oil
small piece of fresh
  ginger root
2 tbs ground
  coriander

½ tsp garam masala or
  curry powder
⅔ cup sour cream
salt and freshly
  ground black pepper
chopped fresh
  cilantro

1 Scrape the carrots and slice them thinly; peel the potatoes and cut them into bigger pieces. Put them into a saucepan, pour over boiling water to cover, then simmer for about 10 minutes, until they are nearly tender.

2 Meanwhile, wash, trim and slice the zucchini. Add them to the pan, along with the frozen peas, and cook for 2–3 minutes, until just tender. Drain the vegetables (keep the water, if you like; it makes excellent soup stock).

3 Heat the oil in a large saucepan, grate the ginger and add it to the pan. Cook for a few seconds, then stir in the ground coriander and garam masala or curry powder and cook for a few seconds more.

4 Add the cooked vegetables and stir over the heat until they are coated with the spices, then stir in the sour cream and continue to cook for a few minutes more until the cream is heated through. Season with salt and pepper and serve sprinkled with chopped cilantro.

SERVES 2

MIXED VEGETABLE CURRY

This makes quite a large quantity and tastes very good the next day, reheated.

1 onion
1 large carrot
2 tbs olive oil
1 large potato, about
  8 ounces
small piece of fresh
  ginger root
1 garlic clove
1 green chili
½ tsp turmeric powder

2 tbs ground
  coriander
¼ tsp curry powder
salt and freshly
  ground black pepper
½ medium cauliflower
4 ounces green beans
fresh cilantro, if
  available

1 Peel and chop the onion; scrape and thinly slice the carrot. Heat the oil in a large saucepan, put in the onion and carrot, then cover and cook gently. Peel the potato, cut it into even-sized pieces and add these to the pan.

2 Grate the ginger and crush the garlic; halve, de-seed and chop the chili. Add these to the pan along with the turmeric, ground coriander and curry powder and stir well for 1–2 minutes so that everything gets coated with the spices.

3 Add 2 cups of water, 2 teaspoons of salt and a grinding of pepper to the pan. Bring to the boil, then leave to simmer, covered, for 5 minutes.

4 Meanwhile, wash the cauliflower and remove the leaves, saving any that are tender; chop these up. Break the cauliflower into flowerets of roughly equal size. Wash and trim the green beans.

5 Stir the cauliflower and beans into the pan then cover and cook for 7–10 minutes or until all the vegetables are just tender. If the mixture looks too liquid, turn up the heat and let it bubble away for a minute or two. Then check the seasoning and serve. It's nice with some fresh cilantro snipped over the top, if you have some.

SERVES 2–4

SPICED SPINACH AND POTATOES

I love the combination of potatoes and dark green leafy vegetables. It's found in a number of peasant dishes around the world. From Ireland there's the soothing Colcannon (see page 100), while India offers this spicy mixture, very different in character yet equally appealing. It's good with some dal (see page 81), if you've time to make that too, otherwise just serve with plain rice or Indian breads.

8 ounces potatoes	1 garlic clove, crushed
2 tbs oil	1 pound tender fresh or
1 red chili, fresh or	frozen spinach
dried	salt and freshly
2 tsp cumin seeds	ground black pepper
½ tsp turmeric	
1 onion, peeled and	
chopped	

1 Peel the potatoes and cut them into ½-inch cubes. Heat the oil in a large saucepan, then put in the whole chili, the cumin seeds and turmeric; stir over the heat for a few seconds, letting the spices fry but not burn.

2 Add the potatoes, onion and garlic then cover and leave them to cook gently for about 15 minutes, or until the potatoes are tender. Stir from time to time and add 1–2 tablespoons of water if the vegetables start to stick.

3 Meanwhile, cook the spinach: if you are using fresh spinach, wash it and put the leaves, still damp, into a large saucepan without any extra water. Cover and cook for 5–8 minutes until tender. If you are using frozen spinach, cook it in ¼ inch of boiling water for about 3 minutes. Drain the spinach well.

4 Add the spinach to the potato mixture and remove the chili. Season with salt and pepper and then serve.

SERVES 2

THAI-FLAVORED EGGPLANT IN COCONUT MILK

Eggplant cooked like this is rich and full of flavor. I like it best served with some plain boiled basmati rice. The eggplant won't spoil if it's cooked ahead of time and reheated – in fact this gives the flavors a chance to develop. Don't leave out the fresh cilantro; it really is essential for this dish.

1 tbs dark sesame oil	salt, freshly ground
1 onion, peeled and	black pepper, and
chopped	sugar
1 garlic clove, crushed	1 bunch of fresh
1 green or red chili	cilantro
1 large eggplant	
1 tbs coconut milk	
powder	

1 Heat the oil in a medium saucepan, add the onion and garlic, then cover and cook gently for 5 minutes, until softened.

2 Meanwhile, halve, de-seed and chop the chili; wash the eggplant and remove the stalk. Cut the eggplant into chunky pieces roughly ½ inch square. Add the chili and eggplant to the pan, then cover and cook for a further 5 minutes. There won't be enough oil for the eggplant to soak up, but that's all right.

3 Put the coconut milk powder into a jug and stir in 1¼ cups of water, then pour this into the pan and bring to the boil. Cover and leave to simmer for about 20 minutes, or until the eggplant is tender and the liquid has reduced to a shiny sauce. If there is too much liquid at this stage, just turn up the heat and let it boil, uncovered, for a few more minutes.

4 Season with plenty of salt and freshly ground black pepper, and some sugar – I find it needs about half a teaspoonful for the right balance of flavors. Then snip in a generous amount of fresh cilantro. You can serve the eggplant straight away, if you like, but it is also extremely good eaten at room temperature.

SERVES 2

You can buy coconut milk powder at Chinese food stores and some large supermarkets. If you can't get it you can substitute 1¼ cups canned coconut milk, or use unsweetened shredded coconut as described on page 85.

FRITTERS & FRIED VEGETABLES

Although most health-conscious people are cutting down on their fat intake, fritters can still have their place in a healthy diet as a delicious occasional treat – and they're quick and easy to make. Serve them with low-fat accompaniments such as salad, steamed vegetables or plain rice.

ONION BHAJEES

A wok is excellent for deep-frying because it has a large surface area but does not require a great deal of oil. Peanut and corn are two of the most suitable oils for deep-frying; but try not to re-use the oil too many times.

These are often served as a nibble, but they make a filling meal served with some plainly cooked rice, chutney and perhaps a raita.

1 cup chick pea (gram) flour	1 tsp salt
2 tsp ground coriander	oil for deep-frying
1 tsp ground cumin	1 onion, peeled and finely chopped
pinch of cayenne pepper	1 tbs chopped fresh cilantro (optional)

1 Sift the chick pea flour into a bowl with the ground coriander, cumin and cayenne. Add the salt, then pour in ⅔ cup of tepid water and stir to make a batter.

2 Heat some oil in a deep-fat fryer or large saucepan. Stir the chopped onion, and the fresh cilantro if you are using this, into the batter, then, when the oil is hot, drop teaspoonfuls of the mixture into the pan and fry, in batches, for about 5 minutes, until they are really crisp and the onion is cooked through.

3 Drain the bhajees on paper towels and keep the first batch warm, uncovered, while you cook the rest. Then serve immediately.

SERVES 2

VEGETABLES IN CHICK PEA BATTER

This is more of a snack than a main meal. Serve with mango chutney and a raita made by stirring fresh cilantro, mint or crushed garlic into plain yogurt.

¾ cup chick pea (gram) flour	1 tsp oil
½ tsp cumin seeds	oil for deep-frying
½ tsp ground coriander	6–8 ounces mixed vegetables: onions, cauliflower and zucchini
good pinch of cayenne pepper	
½ tsp salt	

1 Make the batter: sift the chick pea flour into a bowl then stir in the spices and salt. Add the oil and about ½ cup of warm water to make a fairly thick batter.

2 Heat some oil in a deep-fat fryer, wok or large saucepan. Meanwhile, prepare the vegetables. They need to be in fairly small pieces so that they will have cooked by the time the batter is crisp. Peel onions and slice them into rings; cut cauliflower into fairly small flowerets and zucchini into batons or rounds.

3 Dip the vegetables in the batter and shake off the excess. Fry them in the oil, in batches, for a few minutes, until they are crisp and golden brown on the outside, tender within. Drain on paper towels and serve at once, before they lose their crispness.

SERVES 2

OPPOSITE: *Vegetables in Chick Pea Batter*

MUSHROOMS IN BATTER WITH GARLIC MAYONNAISE

The batter for these is taken from Elizabeth David's French Provincial Cooking, *except that I don't usually let it stand for two hours and certainly not if I'm in a hurry. As Elizabeth David says, it always comes out light and crisp. The mushrooms make a good main course if you serve them with watercress or some other salad.*

1 cup flour	1 garlic clove, crushed
3 tbs olive oil	4 tbs good-quality
salt and freshly	mayonnaise, or
ground black pepper	a mixture of
oil for deep-frying	mayonnaise and
2 cups small white	yogurt
mushrooms; really	1 egg white
tiny ones are best	

1 Sift the flour into a bowl or a food processor, then add the olive oil, 1 teaspoon of salt, a grinding of pepper and ⅔ cup of tepid water. Beat to a smooth cream.

2 Heat some oil in a deep-fat fryer or a large saucepan. Wipe the mushrooms with damp paper towels, then put them on a plate and sprinkle them with salt and a grinding of pepper. Mix the garlic with the mayonnaise or mayonnaise and yogurt.

3 Whisk the egg white until it is stiff then fold it gently into the batter. When the oil is hot, dip the mushrooms into the batter to coat them, then drop them, a few at a time, into the hot oil. Let them fry for about 3–4 minutes, until golden brown and crisp. It's important that they are in the oil long enough to cook through.

4 Drain the mushrooms on paper towels and keep the first lot warm, uncovered, while you cook the rest. Then serve immediately, while they're still really crisp, with the garlic mayonnaise.
SERVES 2–3

Test the temperature of oil for deep-frying by dipping a wooden chopstick or the handle of a wooden spoon into it : if the oil is hot enough it should immediately form bubbles around it.

CHILI AND ONION CORN CAKES

These crisp golden-brown savory cakes make an excellent main course served with a lettuce or tomato salad and some cooked rice. They are also good with chutney, or a sauce made by stirring chopped fresh herbs into plain yogurt.

1¾ cups canned corn	1 green chili
kernels, drained	salt and freshly
1 cup quick-cooking	ground black pepper
polenta	oil for shallow-frying
2 eggs	a little extra grated
⅔ cup grated	Parmesan to serve
Parmesan cheese	(optional)
4 tbs milk	
4 scallions	

1 Put the corn kernels into a bowl with the polenta. Add the eggs, grated Parmesan and milk, and mix together well.

2 Trim and finely chop the scallions; halve, de-seed and finely chop the chili, washing your hands well afterwards. Stir the scallions and chili into the corn mixture and season with salt and pepper.

3 Pour enough oil into a skillet to cover the base thinly. When it is hot, drop heaping tablespoonfuls of the mixture into the pan to make flat 'cakes'. Fry them for about 2 minutes, until crisp and brown underneath, then flip them over and fry the other side for the same amount of time.

4 Drain the cakes on paper towels and keep them warm while you fry the remaining mixture. Serve immediately, sprinkled with some more grated Parmesan, if you like.
SERVES 4

QUICK POTATO PANCAKES

2 large potatoes, about
 1 pound altogether
1 tsp salt

butter
oil

1 Peel the potatoes, then grate them on the coarse side of a grater. Mix the grated potatoes with the salt (don't rinse the potatoes; the starch is necessary to hold the pancakes together).

2 Heat 1 tablespoon of butter and 1 tablespoon of oil in a skillet and put in spoonfuls of the potato mixture, flattening them with the back of the spoon. After about 3 minutes, when the underneath is crisp and brown, turn the pancakes over and cook the other side for about 3 minutes, until brown.

3 Drain on paper towels, then cook the remaining mixture in the same way, adding more butter and oil if necessary. Serve immediately.

SERVES 2

POTATO KOFTAS WITH SPICY BEAN SAUCE

These are crisp potato balls served with a spiced bean mixture.

1 pound potatoes
1 tbs olive oil
1 onion, peeled and
 chopped
1 garlic clove, crushed
1¾ cups canned
 tomatoes
oil for deep-frying
2 tbs lemon juice
3 tbs cornstarch
chili powder

1 tbs chopped fresh
 cilantro
salt, freshly ground
 black pepper, and
 sugar
1 cup dry
 breadcrumbs
1¾ cups canned red
 kidney beans,
 drained
1¾ cups canned corn
 kernels, drained

1 Half-fill a medium-sized pan with water and bring to the boil for the potatoes. Peel the potatoes and cut them into ½-inch cubes. Add them to the water and cook for about 10 minutes, until tender. Drain and mash the potatoes.

2 Start making the sauce: heat the olive oil in a medium pan then fry the onion in it for 5 minutes, until beginning to soften. Stir in the garlic and tomatoes, breaking the tomatoes up roughly with the spoon. Bring to the boil and simmer for 10–15 minutes, until the sauce is very thick with no excess liquid.

3 Start heating some oil for deep-frying, but keep your eye on it. Then finish making the potato koftas: add the lemon juice, cornstarch, a pinch of chili powder, and the chopped cilantro to the potatoes, then season with some salt, pepper and perhaps a pinch of sugar, if necessary.

4 Form the potato mixture into balls about the size of walnuts and roll them in the dry breadcrumbs to coat them lightly.

5 When the oil is hot enough, put in a batch of the koftas and fry for 3–4 minutes, until crisp and golden brown. Drain them on paper towels and keep them warm while you fry the rest.

6 Meanwhile, add the kidney beans and corn kernels to the tomato sauce, then season with salt, pepper, chili powder to taste, and a pinch of sugar, if necessary. Warm over a gentle heat until the beans and corn are heated through. Spoon the bean mixture on to warmed plates, top with the koftas and serve at once.

SERVES 4

The simplest of potato pancakes, quickly made and delicious. Try serving them with sour cream, or apple or cranberry sauce, plus a salad or green vegetable. They are also surprisingly good with hummus.

ROSTI WITH SCALLIONS

Rösti is very quick and simple to prepare and makes a wonderful snack. This version includes scallions but you can vary it by adding different ingredients such as herbs, onion, grated fresh ginger and spices. It's good served with a juicy salad such as tomato and basil, and perhaps some yogurt with fresh herbs stirred into it. Alternatively, serve the crisp rösti with mushrooms in sour cream (see page 106).

1 pound potatoes	*salt*
small bunch of scallions	*4 tbs oil*

1 Scrub the potatoes then put them into a saucepan, cover with cold water and bring to the boil. Boil them for about 5 minutes, until they are just beginning to get tender on the outside. Meanwhile, trim and chop the scallions then cut them into long, thin pieces.

2 Drain the potatoes and leave them until they are cool enough to handle, then slip off the skins using a small sharp knife and your fingers. Grate the potatoes coarsely and season with a little salt, then mix in the scallions.

3 Heat the oil in a skillet, then add the potato mixture and press it down with a spatula to make one large round. Fry over a moderate heat for about 7 minutes, until crisp and brown underneath. Turn the rösti over by turning it out on to a plate then sliding it back into the skillet.

4 Continue to cook the rösti until the second side is browned and crisp, then drain on paper towels, sprinkle with salt and serve at once, cut into wedges.
SERVES 2

OPPOSITE: *(left) Rösti with Scallions, (right) Crisp Fried Eggplant with Parsley Sauce*

CRISP FRIED EGGPLANT WITH PARSLEY SAUCE

I love these crisp slices of eggplant with their creamy sauce. You can serve them just as they are or make more of a meal of them by adding a cooked green vegetable or salad – and even some French fries if you've got time to make them!

1 medium eggplant, about 8 ounces	FOR THE PARSLEY SAUCE
½ cup ground almonds	*2 tbs butter*
1 tsp chopped fresh dill	*2 tbs flour*
1 egg, beaten	*1¼ cups milk*
light olive oil for frying	*4 tbs cream (optional)*
fresh dill to garnish	*2–3 tbs chopped fresh parsley*
	salt and freshly ground black pepper

1 First make the parsley sauce: melt the butter in a saucepan and stir in the flour; when it froths, stir in half the milk, then beat well until it thickens. Stir in the rest of the milk and keep stirring vigorously over the heat, until the sauce is thick and smooth.

2 Let the sauce simmer over a very low heat for about 7 minutes, checking to make sure it doesn't stick or burn. Then stir in the cream, if you're using this, the parsley and plenty of salt and pepper.

3 Wash the eggplant and remove the stalk. Cut the eggplant lengthwise into slices about ¼ inch thick then season with salt and pepper.

4 Mix the ground almonds with the dill and some salt and pepper and put them on a flat plate. Dip the eggplant slices first in beaten egg and then into the ground almond mixture, making sure they are well-coated with almonds on both sides.

5 Heat a little oil in a large skillet, then put in the eggplant slices. You'll probably have to cook them in two batches; turn on the broiler so that you can keep the first batch warm. Fry the eggplant over a moderate heat for about 4 minutes per side, until crisp and golden on both sides and tender inside when pierced with a knife. Drain on paper towels, garnish with dill and serve with the sauce.
SERVES 2

117

STIR-FRIES

—— ✳ ——

THAI STIR-FRY

This stir-fry is delicately flavored with coconut milk but has the added kick of hot red chili and the tang of lemon grass and fresh cilantro. It's delicious with some plain boiled rice; put this on to cook first of all.

If you can't find fresh lemon grass, substitute the grated rind of half a lemon.

⅓ cup unsweetened
  shredded coconut
1 dried red chili
1 large carrot
4 ounces snow peas
4 ounces baby corn
  cobs
1 bunch of scallions
1 red bell pepper
2 tbs peanut oil

½ cup raw peanuts
1 lemon grass stalk
1 garlic clove, crushed
1 cup roughly chopped
  fresh cilantro leaves
salt and freshly
  ground black pepper

To cook plain basmati rice, allow ¼ cup of rice and 1¼ cups of water per person. Wash the rice in a strainer, then bring the water to the boil, pour in the rice and boil fast for about 10 minutes, or until it is tender but still firm. Drain in a strainer and rinse with hot water, then put it back in the pan and keep warm until needed.

1. First prepare the coconut milk: put the shredded coconut in a bowl and cover it with ⅔ cup of boiling water. Leave to infuse.

2. Halve the chili and scrape away and discard the seeds if you prefer less heat. Then chop the chili finely. Scrape the carrot and slice it thinly; top and tail the snow peas, halve the baby corn kernels if they are large; trim and chop the scallions; halve, de-seed and slice the red bell pepper.

3. Strain the coconut through a strainer, pressing it with a wooden spoon. Discard the coconut but keep the liquid. Stir in the red chili.

4. Heat the oil in a wok or very large saucepan. When it is smoking, put in the peanuts and fry them for a few minutes until they smell and look roasted, then add all the vegetables and stir-fry for 1–2 minutes.

5. Finely chop the lemon grass and add it with the garlic to the vegetables; continue to stir-fry for 1–2 minutes until the vegetables are hot but still quite crisp, then pour in the coconut liquid and stir-fry for a few seconds until this is hot. Add the cilantro, season with salt and pepper and serve.
SERVES 2

CHINESE VEGETABLE STIR-FRY

The vegetables suggested here provide a good mixture of colors and textures but you can use different ones if you prefer. Some plain basmati rice goes well with this – put it on to cook before you start preparing the stir-fry.

1 red onion
2 carrots
½ head of Napa
  cabbage
4 ounces broccoli
4 ounces baby corn
  cobs
1 cup small white
  mushrooms
1 tbs peanut oil
1 garlic clove, crushed

small piece of fresh
  ginger root, grated
1 tbs cornstarch
2 tbs good-quality soy
  sauce
1 tsp sugar
good pinch of Chinese
  five-spice powder
salt and freshly
  ground black pepper

1. Peel, halve and slice the onion; scrape the carrots and cut them diagonally into fairly thin slices; wash the Napa cabbage and cut it into fairly chunky slices; separate the broccoli into small flowerets, removing any tough stalk; halve the baby corn cobs if they are large; wash and slice the mushrooms.

2. Heat the oil in a wok or very large saucepan. When it is smoking, put in all the vegetables and the garlic and ginger and stir-fry for 2–3 minutes, until they are wilting but still crunchy.

3. Put the cornstarch into a small bowl or cup and mix with the soy sauce and sugar. Add this to the pan and stir-fry for 1–2 minutes longer, until the mixture has thickened and clings to the vegetables.

4. Add the five-spice powder and some salt and pepper and serve at once.
SERVES 2

OPPOSITE: *Thai Stir-fry*

SNOW PEA AND MUSHROOM STIR-FRY

This is good served simply with some rice, and it also goes well with the red bell pepper and cashew stir-fry, if you want to serve two different dishes for four people.

2 tbs oil
1 large onion, peeled and chopped
small piece of fresh ginger root
1 garlic clove, crushed
8 ounces snow peas
2 cups small white mushrooms

1 tbs cornstarch
1 tsp sugar
1 tbs sherry
1 tbs soy sauce
salt and freshly ground black pepper

1. Heat the oil in a large skillet or wok, put in the onion then cover and cook gently. Grate the ginger and add it to the skillet, along with the garlic.
2. Wash and trim the snow peas and mushrooms as necessary, slicing or halving the mushrooms if they are large.
3. In a cup or small bowl, mix together the cornstarch, sugar, sherry and soy sauce. Leave this on one side for the moment.
4. When the onion is almost done, add the snow peas and mushrooms and stir-fry for 2–3 minutes, until just tender. Then give the soy sauce mixture a quick stir and pour it in; stir until the mixture has thickened and coats the vegetables thinly. Season with salt and pepper, then serve.

SERVES 2

RED BELL PEPPER AND CASHEW STIR-FRY

This is my recreation of a dish I enjoyed in a Chinese restaurant – the combination of soft, sweet peppers and chewy cashews is very good. Serve it with some plain boiled rice.

2 large red bell peppers
2 tbs oil
1 hot red chili, fresh or dried
1 cup cashews

1 tbs cornstarch
1 tbs soy sauce
salt and sugar

1. Halve, de-seed and slice the red bell peppers. Heat the oil in a wok or large saucepan and put in the whole chili; let it sizzle away for a few seconds.
2. Add the peppers and cashews to the pan, cover and cook gently for about 5 minutes, stirring occasionally. Add 1¼ cups of water and cook for a further 10 minutes, until the peppers are very tender.
3. Meanwhile, blend the cornstarch to a paste with the soy sauce, adding a little water if necessary. Pour this into the pepper mixture, stirring until it thickens.
4. Taste, and season with salt and a pinch of sugar if necessary, then serve.

SERVES 2

MAIN-COURSE SALADS

---- ✳ ----

WARM JERUSALEM ARTICHOKE SALAD

This is very filling and makes a good meal for the end of winter or very early spring. The hard-cooked eggs add color, but they can be swapped with Brazil (or other) nuts for a vegan dish.

2 eggs	salt and freshly
1 pound Jerusalem	ground black pepper
artichokes	a few lettuce leaves
1 tbs olive oil	2 tbs snipped fresh
1 tbs balsamic	chives
vinegar	

1. Hard-cook the eggs by simmering them in a pan of boiling water for 7–10 minutes. Then drain them, cover with cold water and leave to cool.
2. Meanwhile, peel the Jerusalem artichokes, dropping them straight into cold water when they're done to keep them white. Then cut them into ¼-inch slices.
3. Heat the oil in a medium saucepan and put in the artichoke slices; shake the pan to coat them with the oil, then cover and leave to cook very gently for about 20 minutes, until they are completely tender.
4. Meanwhile, peel the eggs and cut them into quarters or sixths.
5. Remove the artichokes from the heat, stir in the balsamic vinegar and season with salt and pepper. Arrange the lettuce leaves on a serving plate or two individual plates. Spoon the artichokes on top and sprinkle the chives over them, then arrange the hard-cooked eggs around the edges. Serve at once.

SERVES 2

ITALIAN COUNTRY SALAD

This is a pleasant mixture of flavors and textures. Serve it simply with some country-style bread.

4 eggs	3 tbs olive oil
8 ounces fine green	salt and freshly
beans	ground black pepper
8 ounces zucchini	⅔ cup black olives
1 garlic clove, crushed	2–4 ounces Parmesan
1 tbs red wine vinegar	cheese

1. Hard-cook the eggs by simmering them in a pan of boiling water for 7–10 minutes. Then drain them, cover with cold water and leave to cool.
2. Meanwhile, bring 1 inch of water to the boil in a large saucepan. Wash and trim the beans; wash and slice the zucchini. When the water boils, put in the beans and boil for 1–2 minutes, then add the zucchini and cook for a further 1–2 minutes, until just tender. Drain the vegetables.
3. Put the garlic into a salad bowl with the vinegar, olive oil and some salt and pepper. Mix well, then add the vegetables (which can still be hot). Stir gently.
4. Peel the hard-cooked eggs, then slice them and add them to the bowl, together with the black olives.
5. Cut the Parmesan cheese into thin flakes with a sharp knife or a swivel-bladed vegetable parer and add these to the salad. Toss all the ingredients gently and serve.

SERVES 4

Jerusalem artichokes have such a delicious, almost nutty flavor that it's a pity that many people avoid them because of their anti-social effects on the digestive system... I think their reputation in this respect is a bit exaggerated; anyway, they're certainly worth trying, and enjoying on the right occasions.

GREEN BEAN, AVOCADO AND CASHEW SALAD

This is a rich and filling salad which just needs some good bread to go with it.

1 celery heart
2 small dessert apples
⅔ cup black or red grapes
2 tbs good-quality mayonnaise
2 tbs plain yogurt
salt and freshly ground black pepper
¼ cup walnuts
few leaves of radicchio

1 Wash and slice the celery; peel, core and slice the apples; wash, halve and de-seed the grapes. Put all these ingredients into a bowl with the mayonnaise, yogurt and some salt and pepper to taste and mix gently until combined.
2 Stir in half the walnuts, then spoon the mixture into the radicchio leaves and sprinkle the remaining nuts on top. Serve at once.
SERVES 2

6 ounces thin green beans
1 medium avocado
juice of ½ lemon
1 tbs olive oil
½ cup roasted cashews
salt and freshly ground black pepper

1 Bring ½ inch of water to the boil in a large pan for the green beans. Trim the beans then add them to the boiling water, cover and cook for 2–4 minutes or until just tender. Drain, and put them into a bowl.
2 Halve the avocado, remove the pit and skin, then cut it into long, thin slices.
3 Put the avocado slices into the bowl with the beans and add the lemon juice, olive oil, cashews and a seasoning of salt and pepper. Go easy on the salt if the cashews are already salted. Serve the salad at once.
SERVES 2

THAI CABBAGE SALAD

1 hot red chili
1 lemon grass stalk
8 ounces white cabbage
4 ounces baby corn cobs
1 cup fresh cilantro
1 tbs sesame oil
1 tbs soy sauce
juice of ½ lime
salt and freshly ground black pepper
sugar (optional)

The Thai flavorings in this salad make it quite unusual. Serve it as a side salad with a main dish or with something simple – and most unoriental! – such as broiled cheese on toast.

1 Finely chop the chili, scraping out and discarding the seeds if you prefer. Finely slice the lemon grass, removing any tough stalk, then finely shred the cabbage, slice the baby corn cobs into rounds and chop the cilantro.
2 Heat the oil in a skillet and put in the chili and lemon grass; fry for a few seconds, then add the cabbage and baby corn; stir-fry for 1–2 minutes, until wilted, then remove from the heat, and add the soy sauce and lime juice. Mix well, then lightly stir in the cilantro leaves. Season with salt, pepper and perhaps a pinch of sugar. Serve the salad while still warm.
SERVES 2–4

WALDORF SALAD IN RADICCHIO

This is a light version of the classic Waldorf salad and it includes grapes as well as apples, for a change. It's nicest made with freshly shelled walnuts, if you have time to crack them, and it makes a good lunch or light supper dish, perhaps served with a slice of tea bread or a fruit muffin spread with cream cheese or farmer's cheese.

OPPOSITE: *(top) Green Bean, Avocado and Cashew Salad, (right) Thai Cabbage Salad, (bottom) Waldorf Salad in Radicchio*

FRUIT

*If you're looking for something to give you a
quick burst of energy, fruit beats sugary
convenience foods any day: it's easy to carry,
sweet and delicious to eat, and doesn't make you
fat or rot your teeth. But fruit isn't just for
snacking. It can also be the basis of appetizers,
such as Three-Pear Salad, and light main courses,
such as Apricots with Ricotta and Mint or
Tarragon Pear with Cream Cheese. And, of course,
fruit is perfect for quick nutritious desserts, from
light, refreshing Peaches in Wine or Rhubarb and
Ginger Compote to more substantial puddings
such as Blueberry Crumble.*

FRUIT SALADS & SAVORY FRUIT DISHES

✳

MELON WITH STRAWBERRIES AND MINT

Although most often served as an appetizer, melon makes a pleasant dessert or even a light, refreshing snack. Small round melons with green flesh, such as baby honeydew or Galia, are ideal for this, if you can get them; otherwise use one large melon, cut it into quarters and pile the strawberries on top.

To blanch almonds, put them into a small saucepan, cover with water and boil for 2 minutes, then drain them and pop off the skins with your fingers.

2 cups ripe strawberries
sugar
4 sprigs of mint

16 blanched almonds
2 baby green-fleshed melons, or 1 larger melon

1 Wash and hull the strawberries then cut them into halves or quarters. Put them in a bowl and sprinkle with a little sugar.

2 Roughly tear some mint leaves to release the flavor, and add them to the strawberries, along with the almonds.

3 Cut the baby melons in half or, if you're using one large melon, cut it into quarters. Scoop out and discard the seeds and fill the cavities with the strawberry mixture.
SERVES 4

THREE-PEAR SALAD

Although papayas aren't pears, their shape qualifies them for inclusion in this pretty, refreshing salad, and their flavor combines extremely well with avocado and dessert pears. This is a good appetizer or light lunch dish. Having the fruits perfectly ripe makes all the difference, and it's worth buying them a few days in advance, if necessary, and letting them ripen in a fruit bowl.

1 large ripe dessert pear, preferably Comice
juice of 1 lime
1 large ripe papaya

1 large ripe avocado pear
sprigs of fresh chervil and slices of lime to decorate

1 Cut the pear into quarters then peel and core it. Cut it into long thin slices and sprinkle with a little of the lime juice.

2 Peel and quarter the papaya, scooping out and discarding the seeds, then cut it in the same way as the pear and sprinkle with lime juice.

3 Prepare the avocado similarly, tossing it in the remaining lime juice.

4 Arrange slices of the three 'pears' on individual plates, decorate with the chervil and lime slices and serve as soon as possible.
SERVES 2 AS A LIGHT MEAL, 4 AS AN APPETIZER

OPPOSITE: *(left) Three-Pear Salad, (top) Melon with Strawberries and Mint, (right) Festive Fruit Salad, page 128*

FESTIVE FRUIT SALAD

Fruit with contrasting colors, textures and flavors makes a quick and easy winter dessert with a festive air. Choose whatever fruits you fancy from what is available.

4 clementines	*1 starfruit*
2 persimmons	*1 pomegranate*
12 lichee nuts	

1 Peel the clementines then slice them into rounds and put them into a bowl. Wash the persimmons, remove the stalks and cut the fruit into eighths or smaller sections; add to the bowl.

2 Peel and pit the lichee nuts; wash the starfruit and cut it into thin slices to reveal the starry shapes. Add to the bowl, along with the lichee nuts.

3 Halve the pomegranate then, holding a half over the bowl, scoop out the scarlet seeds with a pointed teaspoon, discarding any tough membranes. Repeat the process with the other half. Stir the seeds gently into the fruit.

SERVES 4

TARRAGON PEAR WITH CREAM CHEESE

This combination is simple but superb, and makes a good light meal or snack. You can control the fat content by your choice of cheese – regular cream cheese, low-fat soft cheese, or cottage cheese are all suitable.

2–3 lettuce leaves	*salt and freshly*
1 perfectly ripe pear,	*ground black pepper*
preferably Comice or	*½ cup soft white*
Bartlett	*cheese*
½ tsp red wine vinegar	*sprig of tarragon*

1 Arrange the lettuce leaves on a serving plate. Cut the pear into quarters, then peel and core it.

Cut the quarters into long, thin slices and arrange these on top of the lettuce leaves.

2 Sprinkle the vinegar over the pear, then top with plenty of coarsely ground black pepper and a less generous scattering of salt – preferably the type you can scrunch up with your fingers.

3 Put the cheese on the plate next to the pear slices, then tear some of the lower leaves from the tarragon over the top and decorate with the tender top part of the tarragon sprig.

SERVES 1

APRICOTS WITH RICOTTA AND MINT

This is only worth doing if you can get really ripe, well-flavored apricots. It makes a lovely light dish, somewhere between an appetizer, salad and a dessert! I like it as a summery lunch or supper when I'm not feeling very hungry.

3–4 ripe apricots	*a little milk or light*
2–3 tsp clear honey	*cream*
½ cup ricotta	*4–6 fresh mint leaves*
cheese	

1 Halve, pit and slice the apricots then put them into a bowl with the honey and mix gently.

2 Put the ricotta cheese into another bowl and mix in enough milk or cream to make a soft, creamy consistency. Then spoon it on top of the apricots but do not cover them completely.

3 Tear the mint leaves roughly and scatter on top. Serve as soon as possible.

SERVES 1

FRESH FRUIT PLATTER

Choose fruits that contrast well in color and texture – figs, kiwis, red currants, raspberries, strawberries, apricots, blueberries and cherries all look good. The more people you are making this for, the more varieties of fruit you can use.

6–8 ounces fresh fruit per person

sprigs of mint, edible blossoms, slivered almonds or crushed pistachios to decorate (optional)

1 Wash and prepare the fruit and cut some in halves or quarters if you like. Figs look especially attractive when quartered.

2 Arrange the fruit on a platter. Decorate, if you wish, with mint sprigs, edible blossoms such as borage or nasturtium, or almonds or pistachios.

ORANGE AND KIWI SALAD

This is a very fresh-looking and fresh-tasting fruit salad, perfect after a rich main course.

2 kiwis
1 large orange
1 tbs orange blossom honey

½ tsp orange flower water

1 Peel the kiwis, then slice them thinly into rounds and put them into a bowl.

2 Holding the orange over the bowl, cut off the peel with a sawing motion, removing all the white pith with the rind. Then cut the sections out from between the membranes and add to the bowl.

3 Add the honey and orange flower water to the fruit and mix gently. Leave in a cool place until ready to serve.

SERVES 1–2

Orange flower water is available from good delicatessens, Middle Eastern stores and supermarkets, but you can leave it out if you can't get it.

COLD DESSERTS
———— ✳ ————

BANANAS WITH CREAM AND SESAME CRISP

You can vary the richness of this, using just thick yogurt or, at the other extreme, just cream. If you don't want to go to the trouble of making the sesame crisp – although it couldn't be easier – buy some sesame crisp bars and use them instead.

2 tbs sesame seeds
6 tbs sugar
⅔ cup heavy cream
⅔ cup thick strained yogurt
4 large bananas

1 First make the sesame crisp: have ready a square of parchment paper. Put the sesame seeds into a small heavy-based saucepan with the sugar and place over the heat. After a minute or so the sugar will melt and then within a few seconds it will turn golden. At this point, remove it from the heat and pour it in a thin layer over the parchment paper. Leave on one side to harden.

2 Whip the cream then fold it carefully into the thick strained yogurt.

3 Peel and slice the bananas, then put them into one large or four individual bowls. Spoon the yogurt cream on top.

4 Peel the paper off the sesame crisp, then crush it into pieces by banging it with a rolling pin; scatter the pieces on top of the bananas and cream.

SERVES 4

HONEYED PEARS WITH ALMOND HALVA

Almond halva, a delicious Middle Eastern confection, can be bought in large supermarkets, delicatessens or Middle Eastern grocery stores. If you can't get it, you could use good-quality nougat instead. Chopped up and sprinkled over ripe fresh fruit, halva makes a good topping, and turns a simple fruit dish into a more substantial dessert. It works best with delicately flavored, sweet fruit such as pears or bananas.

4 large ripe pears, preferably Comice
juice of ½ lemon
3–4 tbs mild honey, clear or thick
3–4 ounces almond halva

1 Cut the pears into quarters then peel and core them. Cut the quarters into long, thin slices, put them into a mixing bowl and toss them in the lemon juice to preserve their color.

2 Put the honey into a pan, judging the amount according to the sweetness of the pears and your own preference. Heat gently until it is liquid, then pour it over the pears. Stir the pears gently and leave on one side until you are ready to serve them.

3 Chop the halva into small pieces. Transfer the pears to one large serving bowl or four individual ones, top with the halva, then serve.

SERVES 4

OPPOSITE: *(left) Fresh Fruit Platter, page 129, (center) Orange and Kiwi Salad, page 129, (right) Bananas with Cream and Sesame Crisp*

RASPBERRIES WITH LEMON SYLLABUB

In this recipe, a tangy syllabub is layered with sweet fresh raspberries. It looks good served in tall glasses – wine glasses are ideal – and other fruit could be used instead of the raspberries. Try it with strawberries, substituting orange for the lemon in the syllabub.

1 cup heavy   2–4 tbs sugar
  cream   1 cup raspberries
grated rind and juice
  of ½ lemon

1 Put the cream into a bowl with the lemon rind and juice and 2 tablespoons of sugar, then whisk until the mixture forms soft peaks. Taste and add more sugar if necessary, remembering that the raspberries will be slightly sharp.

2 Starting with raspberries, layer the raspberries and the lemon syllabub into two tall glasses. Chill until needed.

SERVES 2

STRAWBERRY FOOL

This is a very simple recipe, with the fruit just crushed and then folded into a mixture of yogurt and cream. For a lower-fat version, you could use all yogurt or a larger proportion of yogurt to cream. Other fruits can be substituted: ripe peaches or apricots, for instance.

1½ cups strawberries   ⅔ cup plain yogurt
2–3 tbs sugar
⅔ cup heavy
  cream

1 Wash the strawberries, remove the stalks and slice the fruit roughly. Put it into a large bowl and sprinkle with sugar to taste.

2 Whisk the cream until it stands in soft peaks.

3 Add the yogurt to the strawberries, then mash them into the yogurt with a fork, but don't make the mixture smooth.

4 Fold the whipped cream into the yogurt and strawberries. Taste, and gently stir in a little more sugar if necessary.

SERVES 2–3

FRESH PINEAPPLE FOOL

You really need a sweet, well-flavored pineapple for this recipe – choose a ripe, strongly scented one. It is tempting to make a lower-fat version using half cream and half yogurt, but I don't find that it works as well – yogurt is fairly acidic, whereas the richness of heavy cream balances the natural sharpness of the pineapple.

1 ripe pineapple   1¼ cups heavy cream
juice of 1 orange   chopped pistachio
2 tbs sugar, or to   nuts or fresh mint
  taste   leaves to decorate
2 tbs orange liqueur,   (optional)
  such as Cointreau or
  Grand Marnier

1 Peel the pineapple, removing all the tufts and the hard inner core, then chop it fairly finely or purée it in a food processor.

2 Add the orange juice to the pineapple and sprinkle with the sugar and the liqueur.

3 Whip the cream until it forms soft peaks – the acidity of the pineapple will firm it up a bit, so don't make it too stiff. Then fold the pineapple gently into the cream. Taste, and sweeten with a little more sugar if necessary.

4 Spoon the mixture into tall glasses or individual bowls and chill well before serving. Decorate with chopped pistachio nuts or fresh mint leaves, if you like.

SERVES 4

FRUIT AND ICE-CREAM

Good-quality store-bought ice-cream, mixed with fresh fruit and other extras such as nuts, alcohol, chocolate or coffee, makes an almost instant dessert that is popular with most people. Decent vanilla ice-cream goes with almost any fruit, and good fruit sorbets are also useful. More strongly flavored ice-creams, such as chocolate or ginger, can be very effective if you pair them with the right fruit. Here are some ideas.

1 VANILLA ICE-CREAM WITH MELON AND GINGER

If you can get ripe, sweet baby melons, serve them cut in half and topped with a scoop of vanilla ice-cream, some chopped preserved stem ginger and some of its syrup. Or you could use a larger melon cut into pieces.

2 VANILLA ICE-CREAM WITH RUM RAISINS AND HOT CHOCOLATE SAUCE

For each person, put 1 tablespoon of raisins and 1 tablespoon of rum into a small pan and heat gently, then leave on one side to steep. Make the chocolate sauce (see page 140). Let the ice-cream soften at room temperature while you eat your main course then fold the raisins and rum into the ice-cream and pour the chocolate sauce over the top.

3 VANILLA ICE-CREAM WITH BANANAS AND COFFEE

Make some espresso coffee. Slice a banana into a bowl, top with a scoop of vanilla ice-cream then pour the hot coffee over the top. Some whipped cream is good with this, too.

4 VANILLA ICE-CREAM WITH ARMAGNAC PRUNES

Allow about 4 prunes for each serving – they should be the plump, ready-to-eat type. Put them into a shallow dish and sprinkle with 1 tablespoon of Armagnac or cognac, then leave them to steep – the longer you can leave them the better. Serve with a scoop of vanilla ice-cream and some toasted slivered almonds, if you like.

5 LEMON SORBET WITH RASPBERRY SAUCE

Make the raspberry sauce (see page 136). Pour a pool of sauce on to each plate and top with some good-quality lemon sorbet.

6 MANGO SORBET WITH EXOTIC FRUITS

Make store-bought mango sorbet into a festive dessert by serving it in scoops surrounded by pieces of exotic fruit: mango, lichee nuts, papaya, persimmon, physalis – whatever is available. Passion fruit sorbet is also good served like this.

7 CHOCOLATE ICE-CREAM WITH PEARS, CHERRIES OR ORANGES

Serve scoops of rich chocolate ice-cream with any of these fruits, perhaps tossed with a little liqueur or eau de vie: poire William for pears, kirsch for cherries (they should be juicy dark ones, with the stones removed), Grand Marnier or Cointreau for oranges. Strawberries are also good: marinate these in an orange-flavored liqueur.

8 COFFEE ICE-CREAM WITH PEARS AND MAPLE SYRUP

Peel and slice a ripe pear for each person; top with scoops of softened coffee ice-cream, drizzle over some maple syrup, and sprinkle with chopped pecans.

9 STRAWBERRY ICE-CREAM WITH PEACHES AND AMARETTI

Peel and slice a large ripe peach for each person; top with a scoop of strawberry ice-cream and some softly whipped cream, then sprinkle over 2–3 crushed amaretti cookies.

When you buy maple syrup, read the label to make sure it's the real stuff and not 'maple-flavored syrup.' It's expensive but a little goes a long way and it keeps very well in the fridge.

RHUBARB AND GINGER COMPOTE

Fresh-tasting and succulent, this is good with almond- or orange-flavored biscuits and some thick yogurt or cream. It can be served either cold or hot.

2 pieces of stem ginger
  preserved in syrup
2 pounds rhubarb

4 tbs sugar
4 tbs ginger syrup from
  the jar

1. Finely chop the ginger. Trim the rhubarb and remove any stringy bits then cut it into 1-inch lengths. Wash these, then put them into a pan with the sugar, ginger syrup and chopped ginger, reserving some ginger for decoration.
2. Cover and let cook very gently for 2–3 minutes. Stir gently, then cook for a further 2–3 minutes, until the rhubarb is tender. Decorate with the reserved chopped ginger before serving.
SERVES 4

FRESH FRUIT MUESLI

We usually think of muesli as a cereal-based breakfast dish, but the original version was served for supper and was prepared mostly of fruit, usually grated apple. Made like this, with the addition of honey, nuts and plain yogurt, muesli makes a good dessert or, as I sometimes like to eat it, a complete lunch or supper dish.

2 tbs raisins
⅔ cup plain yogurt
1–1 ½ tbs clear
  honey
1 tbs rolled oats

1 large sweet apple or
  pear
2 tbs toasted slivered
  almonds or hazelnuts
light cream (optional)

1. Put the raisins into a small bowl, cover with a little boiling water and leave to plump up.
2. Put the yogurt into a bowl and add 1 tablespoon of the honey and the oats.

3. Wash the apple or pear then grate it quite coarsely into the bowl on top of the yogurt. Drain the raisins and add them to the bowl, then gently stir everything together.
4. Top with the almonds or hazelnuts. You can drizzle a little more honey over the top if you want to make it sweeter, and serve with some light cream for a richer version.
SERVES 1

MARINATED NECTARINES AND RASPBERRIES

A quick but good summer dessert. Unless the fruit is particularly sweet, I think it needs a little help – you could use either sugar or a mild, clear honey, whichever you prefer.

2 ripe nectarines
2 cups fresh
  raspberries
2–4 tbs sugar, or a
  little clear honey

1–2 tbs kirsch, eau de
  framboise or eau de
  vie (optional)

1. Halve, pit and slice the nectarines then put them into a bowl. Wash the raspberries gently, then add them to the bowl.
2. Add sugar or honey to taste, and the liqueur if you're using this. Stir gently, then leave to marinate for 15–30 minutes.
SERVES 2–3

OPPOSITE: *Rhubarb and Ginger Compote*

PEACHES IN WINE

Ideally this should be made ahead to give the flavors time to develop, so prepare it before you start making the rest of the meal. Light cookies and some thick creamy yogurt, lightly whipped cream or good-quality vanilla ice-cream go well with it.

4–6 large ripe peaches   **sugar**
1¼ cups sweet white
  wine

1 Put the peaches into a bowl, cover them with boiling water for 2 minutes, until the skins loosen, then slip off the skins with a sharp knife.

2 Halve, pit and thinly slice the peaches. Put them into a bowl – a pretty glass one looks good – and pour over the wine.

3 Sweeten the mixture with a little sugar to taste, then cover the bowl and chill for as long as possible before serving.

SERVES 4

STRAWBERRIES IN RASPBERRY SAUCE

This is an ideal dessert to make in the early summer, when strawberries are at their best. You can use frozen raspberries for the sauce if fresh ones aren't available.

2 cups raspberries   **3 cups strawberries**
2 tbs sugar, or to
  taste

1 Purée the raspberries in a food processor then pass them through a nylon strainer to remove the seeds. Stir in the sugar.

2 Wash and hull the strawberries, then slice them. Mix the strawberries with the raspberry sauce; taste, and add more sugar if necessary.

SERVES 4

Strawberries in raspberry sauce are good on their own or with a dollop of thick strained yogurt or crème fraîche and some crisp delicate cookies.

FRUITS IN LIQUEUR OR BRANDY

Marinating ripe fresh fruits in liqueur, brandy or eau de vie is a great way to turn them into a dessert. The longer you leave them to soak the better; if you prepare them before you start making the rest of the meal the flavors will have a chance to emerge. Choose really ripe, sweet fruit.

TRY THE FOLLOWING
COMBINATIONS:
Pineapple (make sure
  it is really ripe) or
  black cherries with
  kirsch
Oranges, clementines
  or tangerines, peeled
  and sliced into thin
  rings, with an orange
  liqueur such as
  Grand Marnier

Strawberries with
  orange liqueur
Peaches with brandy
Plums with Amaretto
  (the plums must be
  very sweet and ripe)
Pear (my favorite)
  preferably a perfectly
  ripe Comice, peeled,
  sliced and sprinkled
  with poire William
  liqueur

1 Peel, trim, core and slice the fruit as necessary – the smaller the pieces, the more they'll absorb the flavors.

2 Put the fruit into a bowl, sweeten with a little sugar to taste and pour over a few tablespoons of your chosen alcohol.

3 You can add extras just before serving, such as a sprinkling of pistachio nuts, slivered almonds or some flakes of chocolate. Serve accompanied by yogurt, cream and/or cookies if you like.

GRAPES IN BEAUMES DE VENISE

This is good served in large wine glasses – so you can drink the last drops of delicious juice! It doesn't really need any accompaniment, although you could consider serving delicate, almondy cookies with it.

2 cups sweet grapes, white or a mixture of white, red and black

about ⅔ cup Beaumes de Venise or other sweet dessert wine

1   Wash and halve the grapes and remove the seeds. Put the grapes into two glasses or a glass serving bowl.

2   Pour the wine over the grapes and leave until you are ready to serve – but don't chill them as this dulls the flavor.
SERVES 2

MELON, GINGER AND KIWI COMPOTE

This is a very good way of improving the flavor of a melon that isn't as sweet as it might be. Ginger jam is used for flavoring and sweetening – or you could use chopped preserved ginger from a jar, with some of the syrup.

1 medium-sized melon   **4 kiwis**
4 tbs ginger jam

1   Halve the melon and remove the seeds, then chop the flesh into pieces and put them into a bowl with the ginger jam.

2   Peel the kiwis and cut them into fairly thin slices; add these to the bowl. Stir, then leave until you are ready to serve the dessert – the longer you can leave it, the more the flavors will develop.
SERVES 4

TANGERINES IN CARAMEL SAUCE

This is a quick and easy way of dressing up tangerines for an elegant dessert. You can, of course, use other members of the tangerine family, such as clementines or mandarins – if they are small you'll need more than four. Very small ones look pretty peeled and served whole on top of the sauce.

¾ cup sugar   **4 large tangerines**

1   Put half the sugar into a small saucepan and heat gently until it melts and becomes caramel colored – this will take several minutes.

2   Standing well back and covering your hand with a cloth, pour in 2 tablespoons of water; the mixture will erupt and turn lumpy.

3   Add the remaining sugar and continue to cook over a gentle heat until the sauce has become smooth again.

4   Leave the sauce on one side to cool slightly while you peel the tangerines and slice them into thin rounds, if they are large. Then pour the sauce on to four plates, top with the tangerines and serve.
SERVES 4

HOT DESSERTS

HOT HONEY PEACHES WITH AMARETTI

This is a good way of cheering up peaches – or indeed other fruits, such as apricots or pears – that are not as sweet and juicy as they might be. They are good with some thick strained yogurt.

1–2 peaches	*2–3 amaretti cookies*
2–3 tsp mild honey,	
clear or thick	

1 Slice the peaches finely, peeling them first if you prefer, then put them into a small pan, add honey to taste and heat gently.

2 Let the peach slices cook over a low heat for a few more minutes until they are sweet and tender, then serve them straight away with the amaretti cookies: either leave them whole or crush them and sprinkle them over the peaches.
SERVES 1

BUTTERED APPLES

Mellow dessert apples such as Cortland, Baldwin or really tasty Golden Delicious, if you can get them, work best in this recipe – and sweet, ripe pears are also good. It's best served hot, with thick creamy yogurt and perhaps an almond- or orange-flavored cookie.

1 pound mellow	*2 tsp sugar*
apples	*⅓ cup golden raisins*
1 tbs butter	

1 Peel and quarter the apples, remove the cores, then cut each quarter into thin slices.

2 Melt the butter in a saucepan and add the apples, sugar and golden raisins. Stir, then cook, uncovered, over a gentle heat for 3–4 minutes, stirring gently from time to time, until the apples have heated through and softened. Serve at once.
SERVES 2

QUICK BLUEBERRY CRUMBLE

A crumble is the most popular of desserts and also one of the quickest to prepare. To speed up the cooking, this one is broiled instead of baked, producing a really good crisp topping. You can use many other types of fruit instead of blueberries. Choose soft fruit that doesn't need pre-cooking.

1½ cups blueberries	*½ cup butter*
1¼ cups flour	*1 tbs slivered almonds*
½ cup sugar	

1 Wash the blueberries then put them into a shallow heatproof dish. Heat the broiler to medium.

2 To make the crumble, put the flour and sugar into a bowl and rub in the butter with your fingertips. Or whizz all these ingredients together in a food processor fitted with a plastic blade.

3 Arrange the crumble on top of the blueberries and broil for 10–15 minutes or until the crumble is brown and the blueberries bubbling. If the crumble seems to be browning too quickly, cover the dish with aluminum foil. Scatter the almonds over the crumble 2–3 minutes before it is ready, removing the foil, if you are using it, so that they brown.
SERVES 2–3

OPPOSITE: *(top) Buttered Apples, (bottom) Quick Blueberry Crumble*

BANANAS OR PEARS WITH HOT CHOCOLATE SAUCE

Chocolate sauce is quick to make and turns bananas or pears into a hot dessert when you want something simple and easy but a bit special.

4 ounces semisweet
  chocolate
1 tbs sweet butter
4 medium bananas
  or sweet ripe
  pears

a few slivered almonds
whipped cream
  (optional)

The better the chocolate, the better the sauce... one with at least 50 percent cocoa solids is best (read the packet) though you don't want too bitter a chocolate for this recipe.

1 First make the chocolate sauce: break up the chocolate and put it into a small saucepan with the butter and ⅓ cup of water. Heat gently until the chocolate has melted.
2 Peel and slice the bananas, or peel, core and slice the pears. Arrange in four individual dishes.
3 Give the chocolate sauce a stir then pour it over the fruit just before you want to serve it. Top with a few slivered almonds, and a little whipped cream if you are using this.
SERVES 4

FLAMBEED FRUIT

This is good made with tropical fruits: bananas and pineapple work particularly well. It's quite dramatic when the flames go up, so stand well back.

1 small ripe pineapple
2 large bananas
2 tbs sweet butter
2 tbs brown sugar
juice of 1 orange

4 tbs dark rum
toasted flaked coconut
  or toasted slivered
  almonds (optional)

1 Peel the pineapple, removing the tufts and hard core, then cut it into medium-sized chunks. Peel and slice the bananas.

2 Melt the butter and sugar in a saucepan then add the fruit and orange juice. Cook, stirring, for 3–4 minutes, until the fruit is heated through.
3 Put the rum into a small saucepan or metal ladle and warm it over a flame or the stove. When it is tepid, set it alight with a match, standing well back and averting your face. Tip it into the fruit and let it burn, then serve immediately, sprinkled with the toasted coconut or almonds.
SERVES 4

INDIVIDUAL BANANA AND ALMOND CRUMBLES

4 large bananas
1 cup flour
½ cup ground
  almonds
2 tbs softened
  butter

4 tbs light brown
  sugar
¼ cup slivered
  almonds

1 Heat the broiler to medium. Peel the bananas and slice each one fairly thinly into a ramekin dish.
2 Sift the flour into a bowl. Add the ground almonds, butter and sugar and mix them to a crumbly consistency with a fork. Then mix in the slivered almonds.
3 Spoon the crumble on top of the bananas then broil for 10–15 minutes, until the topping is crisp and brown and the bananas are heated through. If the crumble is getting too brown before the bananas are hot, cover with some aluminum foil.
SERVES 4

ORANGE ZABAGLIONE WITH STRAWBERRIES

You can whizz up this luxurious dessert in no time at all with a hand electric beater; without one it takes a little longer. Ladyfingers or delicate thin almond cookies go well with it.

1–1½ cups strawberries	1 tbs orange liqueur, such as Cointreau
3 tbs sugar	slivers of orange rind to decorate
2 egg yolks	
grated rind of ½ orange	

1 Set a heatproof bowl over a pan of water and heat until the water is steaming. Make sure the bowl is not touching the water in the pan.

2 Wash and hull the strawberries then halve or slice them. Divide them between two bowls, sprinkle with 1 tablespoon of the sugar and leave on one side.

3 Put the egg yolks into the bowl and add the remaining sugar and the grated orange rind. Keeping the bowl over the pan of steaming water, whisk until pale and thick: about 5 minutes with an electric beater, 10–15 minutes by hand.

4 Stir in the orange liqueur, then spoon the zabaglione over the strawberries, decorate with a few slivers of orange rind, and serve at once.
SERVES 2

BANANA FRITTERS WITH LIME

oil for deep-frying	3 bananas
1 cup flour	sugar
1 tbs melted butter	1 lime, sliced
1 egg white	crème fraîche

1 Set the oven to 300°F (150°C). Heat some oil for deep-frying in a saucepan.

2 Next make the batter: sift the flour into a bowl, make a well in the center and add the butter and ⅔ cup of water. Mix until smooth. Whisk the egg white until it is standing in stiff peaks, then fold it into the batter.

3 Peel the bananas and cut them into chunks. Dip them into the batter, drain off the excess and fry in the hot oil, a few at a time, for 2–3 minutes, turning them over half way through.

4 Drain the fritters on paper towels and keep them warm in the oven while you fry the rest. As soon as they are all done, serve the fritters sprinkled with sugar and decorated with slices of lime. Serve the crème fraîche separately in a small bowl.
SERVES 4

PLUMS WITH CINNAMON CRUNCH

This quick, unconventional topping goes well with many types of cooked fresh fruit.

2 pounds red plums	1 cup rolled oats
¾ cup raw cane sugar or brown sugar	1 tsp cinnamon
3 tbs butter	pinch of ground cloves

1 Halve and pit the plums, then cut them into chunky slices. Put them into a saucepan with 2 tablespoons of water and two thirds of the sugar and cook gently until the sugar has melted and the plums are just tender.

2 Preheat the broiler. Melt the butter in a separate pan, then stir in the oats and the remaining sugar. Mix well, then spread the mixture on a broiler pan or cookie sheet and broil for about 10 minutes, stirring often, until the mixture is brown and crisp. Stir in the cinnamon and cloves.

3 Reheat the plums, then transfer them to a pie dish that will fit under your broiler, spread the oat mixture on top, and keep warm under the broiler until you are ready to serve.
SERVES 4

INDEX

※